HOW TO DEVELOP A
PERFECT MEMORY

Dominic O'Brien is the current World Memory Champion and holds two *Guinness Book of Records* entries for memorizing the sequence of thirty-five packs of shuffled cards and a single pack of cards in the staggering time of 55.62 seconds. He became interested in memory in 1988 when he saw a pack of cards memorized on TV's *Record Breakers* and was further inspired by Dustin Hoffman's character in the film *Rainman*. In 1991 he competed in the first World Memory Championship in London, and won, beating the card memorizer who had first prompted him to develop his own memory system.

How To Develop
A
Perfect Memory

Dominic O'Brien

HEADLINE

The *Father of the Bride* speech by Richard Curtis and
Rowan Atkinson is reproduced by kind permission of
The Peters, Fraser & Dunlop Group Ltd and PJB Management.

Dominic O'Brien's Management Company:
Bob England, Hurricane, 17 Bull Plain, Hertford,
Herts SG14 1DX. Tel: 0992 500818

First published in 1993
by Pavilion Books Limited

First published in paperback in 1994
by HEADLINE BOOK PUBLISHING

10 9 8 7 6 5 4 3 2 1

ISBN 0 7472 4517 7

Typeset by
Letterpart Limited, Reigate, Surrey
Printed and bound in Great Britain by
HarperCollins Manufacturing, Glasgow

HEADLINE BOOK PUBLISHING
A division of Hodder Headline PLC
338 Euston Road, London NW1 3BH

To my dear mother Pamela who is forever saying,
'How *does* he do it!'

The author would like to thank Jon Stock for his
invaluable assistance in preparing this book.

Contents

1   Introduction   1
2   How to remember lists   6
3   What's in a name?   19
4   How to remember numbers   35
5   The mental diary   56
6   The mental in-tray   65
7   Memory and job interviews   68
8   How to remember speeches   72
9   How to remember directions   77
10 Learning the twentieth-century calendar   84
11 How to remember 'lost' chapters of your life   99
12 How to learn languages   104
13 How to remember geographical facts   114
14 How to remember history   128
15 Popular mnemonics   141
16 How to memorize a pack of playing cards   149
17 How to win (always) at *Trivial Pursuit*   163
18 Memory and sport   171
19 How memory can improve your golf swing   181
20 How memory can improve your chess game   187
21 How to memorize thirty-five decks   197
22 Number crunching   201

23 Remembering binary numbers   211
24 How to win at blackjack   219
25 How to beat quiz machines   233
26 Memory and the Greeks   243
27 Famous memory men   255
28 Conclusion   273

Bibliography   275

CHAPTER 1

• •

Introduction

I know what it is like to forget someone's name. In my time, I have forgotten appointments, telephone numbers, speeches, punchlines of jokes, directions, even whole chapters of my life. Up until recently, I was the most absent-minded, forgetful person you could imagine. I once saw a cartoon of two people dancing rather awkwardly at the Amnesiacs' Annual Ball. The man was saying to the woman, 'Do I come here often?' I knew how he felt.

Within the last four years, I have become the World Memory Champion. I regularly appear on television and tour the country as a celebrity 'Memory Man', rather like Leslie Welch did in the 1950s. There's no trickery in what I do – no special effects or electronic aids. I just sat down one day and decided enough was enough: I was going to train my memory.

LEARNING HOW TO USE YOUR BRAIN

Imagine going out and buying the most powerful computer in the world. You stagger home with it, hoping that it will do everything for you, even write your letters. Unfortunately, there's no instruction

1

manual and you don't know the first thing about computers. So it just sits there on the kitchen table, staring back at you. You plug it in, fiddle around with the keyboard, walk around it, kick it, remember how much money it cost. Try as you might, you can't get the stupid thing to work. It's much the same with your brain.

The brain is more powerful than any computer, far better than anything money can buy. Scientists barely understand how a mere 10 per cent of it works. They know, however, that it is capable of storing and recalling enormous amounts of information. If, as is now widely accepted, it contains an estimated 10^{12} neurons, the number of possible combinations between them (which is the way scientists think information is stored) is greater than the number of particles in the universe. For most of us, however, the memory sits up there unused, like the computer on the kitchen table.

There are various ways of getting it to work, some based on theory, some on practice. What you are about to read is a method I have developed independently over the last five years.

Throughout this book, you will be asked to create images for everything you want to remember. These images will come from your imagination; often bizarre, they are based on the principles of association (we are reminded of one thing by its relation to another). Don't worry that your head may become too cluttered by images. They are solely a means of making information more palatable for your memory and will fade once the data has been stored.

It is essential, however, that you form your own images. I have given examples throughout the book, but they are not meant to be copied verbatim. Your own inventions will work much better for you than mine.

BETTER QUALITY OF LIFE

I have a stubborn streak, which kept me going through the long hours of trial and error, and I am pleased to say that my method is all grounded in personal experience. Those techniques that didn't work were altered until they did, or thrown out. In other words, the method works, producing some remarkable results in a short space of time.

The most dramatic change has been the improvement in the overall quality of my life. And it's not just the little things, like never needing to write down phone numbers or shopping lists. I can now be introduced to a hundred new people at a party and remember all their names perfectly. Imagine what that does for your social confidence.

My memory has also helped me to lead a more organized life. I don't need to use a diary any more: appointments are all stored in my head. I can give speeches and talks without referring to any notes. I can absorb and recall huge amounts of information (particularly useful if you are revising for exams or learning a new language). And I have used my memory to earn considerable amounts of money at the blackjack table.

WHAT I HAVE DONE, YOU CAN DO

Some people have asked me whether they need to be highly intelligent to have a good memory, sensing that my achievements might be based on an exceptional IQ. It's a flattering idea, but not true. Everything I have done could be equally achieved by anyone who is prepared to train their memory.

I didn't excel at school. Far from it. I got eight mediocre O levels and dropped out before taking any A levels. I couldn't concentrate in class and I wasn't an avid reader. At one point, my teachers thought I was dyslexic. I was certainly no child prodigy. However, training my memory has *made* me more switched on, mentally alert, and observant than I ever was.

REASSURING PRECEDENTS

During the course of writing this book, I have discovered that my method bears many similarities with the classical art of memory. The Greeks, and later the Romans, possessed some of the most awesome memories the civilized world has ever seen.

There are also some striking resemblances between my approach and the techniques used by a Russian named Shereshevsky but known simply as S. Born at the end of the nineteenth century he was a constant source of bewilderment and fascination for Russian psychologists. To all intents and purposes, he had a limitless memory.

I can't help thinking that there must be validity in my method when such similar techniques have been developed independently of each other by people from such different cultures and times.

PRACTICE MAKES PERFECT

No method, however, produces results unless you are prepared to put in a little time and effort. The more you practise the techniques I describe, the quicker you will become at applying them. And remember, an image or a thought that might take a paragraph to describe can be created in a nanosecond by the human brain. Have faith in your memory and see this book as your instruction manual, a way of getting it to work.

. . . .

CHAPTER 2

How to remember lists

A TRIP DOWN MEMORY LANE

A list of ten items, whatever they are, should not present a challenge to our memory, and yet it does. Take a simple shopping list, for example. Try memorizing the following within one minute, without writing any of it down.

- fish
- margarine
- chess set
- milk
- light bulb
- football
- ladder
- clock
- tape measure
- dog bowl

Most people can remember somewhere between four and seven items. And there was I announcing in the introduction that you have an amazing memory. It wasn't an idle boast. By the end of this chapter, you should be able to remember any ten items perfectly in order, even backwards in under one minute. To prove my point, try doing the following two simple exercises.

Remembering the forgettable

Think back over what you have done so far today. What time did you get up? What was on the radio or television? Can you remember your journey into work?

What mood were you in when you arrived? Did you go anywhere on foot, or in a car? Whom did you meet?

Frustrating, isn't it? Your memory has no problem at all recalling these everyday, mundane experiences (ironically, the forgettable things in life) and yet it can't recall a simple shopping list when required. If you were to take this exercise a stage further and write down *everything* you could remember about today, however trivial or tedious, you would be amazed at the hundreds of memories that came flooding back.

Some things are undoubtedly easier to remember than others, events that involve travel, for example. When I think back over a day, or perhaps a holiday, the most vivid memories are associated with a journey. Perhaps I was on a train, or walking through the park, or on a coach; I can remember what happened at certain points along the way. A journey gives structure to the otherwise ramshackle collection of memories in your head; it helps you to keep them in order, like a filing cabinet.

Remembering the sublime

If, like me, you found the first exercise a little depressing, revealing more about the ordinariness of your life than about your memory, you should enjoy this experiment. Try to *imagine* a day. Exaggerate and distort your normal routine . . .

Wake up in an enormous, feathersoft bed to the sound of birdsong; a beautiful lover is lying asleep beside you; pull back the curtains to reveal sun-soaked

7

hills rolling down to a sparkling sea. An enormous schooner is at anchor in the bay, its fresh, white linen sails flapping in the Mediterranean breeze. Breakfast has been made; the post comes and, for once, you decide to open the envelope saying 'You have won a £1 million'. You have! etc, etc.

Your dream day might be quite different from mine, of course. But if you were to put this book down and I were to ask you in an hour's time to recall the fruits of your wild imagination, you should be able to remember everything you dreamt up. Imagined events are almost as easy to recall as real ones, particularly if they are exaggerated and pleasurable. (No one likes to remember a bad dream.) This is because the imagination and memory are both concerned with the forming of mental images.

Returning from the sublime to the ridiculous, you are now in a position to remember the ten items on our shopping list, armed with the results of these two experiments. Keep an open mind as you read the following few paragraphs.

THE METHOD

To remember the list, 'place' each item of shopping at individual stages along a familiar journey – it might be around your house, down to the shops, or a bus route.

For these singularly boring items to become memorable, you are going to have to exaggerate them, creating bizarre mental images at each stage of the journey. Imagine an enormous, gulping fish flapping around your bedroom, for example, covering the duvet with slimy scales. Or picture a bath full of margarine; every time you turn on the taps, more warm margarine comes oozing out!

This is the basis of my entire memory system:

THE KEY TO A PERFECT MEMORY IS YOUR IMAGINATION

Later on, when you need to remember the list, you are going to 'walk' around the journey, moving from stage to stage and recalling each object as you go. The journey provides order, linking items together. Your imagination makes each one memorable.

The journey

Choose a familiar journey. A simple route around your house is as good as any. If there are ten items to remember, the journey must consist of ten stages. Give it a logical starting point, places along the way and a finishing point. Now learn it. Once you have committed this to memory, you can use it for remembering ten phone numbers, ten people, ten appointments, ten of anything, over and over again.

Your map:

Stage 1:	your bedroom	*Stage 6:*	kitchen
Stage 2:	bathroom	*Stage 7:*	front door
Stage 3:	spare room	*Stage 8:*	front garden
Stage 4:	stairs	*Stage 9:*	road
Stage 5:	lounge	*Stage 10:*	house opposite

At each stage on the map, close your eyes and visualize your own home. For the purposes of demonstration, I have chosen a simple two-up, two-down house. If you live in a flat or bungalow, replace the stairs with a corridor or another room. Whatever rooms you use, make sure the journey has a logical direction. For instance, I would not walk from my bedroom through the front garden to get to the bathroom. The sequence must be obvious. It then becomes much easier to preserve the natural order of the list you intend to memorize.

If you are having difficulty, try to imagine yourself floating through your house, visualizing as much of the layout at each stage as you can. Practise this a few times. When you can remember the journey without having to look at your map, you are ready to attempt the shopping list itself. This time, I hope, with markedly different results.

That shopping list again:

Item 1:	fish	*Item 6:*	football
Item 2:	margarine	*Item 7:*	ladder
Item 3:	chess set	*Item 8:*	clock
Item 4:	milk	*Item 9:*	tape measure
Item 5:	light bulb	*Item 10:*	dog bowl

Bizarre images

Using your imagination, you are going to repeat the journey, but this time 'placing' each object at the corresponding stage. The intention, remember, is to create a series of bizarre mental images, so out of the ordinary that you can't help remembering them. Have you ever seen chess pieces standing six feet high and shouting at each other, in your spare room? And what are all those hundreds of smashed milk bottles doing on the stairs?

Make the scenes as unusual as possible. Use all your senses; taste, touch, smell, hear and see everything. The more senses you can bring to bear, the more memorable the image will be. (For instance, if we want to remember a word on a page, we often say it out loud.) Movement is also important, and so is sex.

Don't be embarrassed by your own creativity. There are no rules when it comes to exploring your imagination. You are the only member of the audience. Shock yourself! You will remember the scene more vividly. The more wild and exaggerated, the easier it will be to remember. Let your imagination run riot; it is the only thing limiting your memory.

Placing the objects

To show you what I mean, here is how I would memorize the list:

STAGE 1:
> I wake up in my bedroom to find that I am holding a fishing rod. At the end of the line is a huge slimy fish frantically at the foot of my bed.

I use all my senses: I see the rod arcing, I hear the spool clicking, I feel the pull of the line, I smell the foul, fishy odour, I touch its scales.

STAGE 2:
> I go to the bathroom to take a shower. Instead of hot

water, a thick margarine oozes from the showerhead and drips all over me.

I feel the warm, sticky texture and see the bright, fluorescent yellow colour.

STAGE 3:

I walk into the spare room and discover a giant chess set. Like something out of *Alice's Adventures in Wonderland*, the pieces are coming alive.

I can hear them shouting obscenities at each other, insulting each other's king and queen.

STAGE 4:

The staircase is cluttered with hundreds of milk bottles, some of them half empty, even broken. The milkman is standing at the bottom of the stairs, apologizing for the mess.

I pick my way down the stairs, smelling the stench of decaying milk. I hear the noise of crunching glass, and the squelch of curdled milk underfoot. What was the milkman doing there in the first place? The more mental 'hooks' and associations you gather, the greater your chances of recalling the item.

STAGE 5:

I open the lounge door. Instead of seeing the light bulb dangling unobtrusively from the ceiling, it is sprouting from out of the floor, huge and growing bigger by the minute.

I walk around it, feel the heat its enormous filament is generating, raise my hands to protect my eyes from the glare. The bulb explodes and shatters into a million myriad pieces. A sudden violent experience is always memorable. It is important, however, to vary the scenes; overuse or repetition of a particular dramatic effect will only confuse you.

STAGE 6:

   A football match is in progress in the kitchen. Crockery and ornaments lie smashed on the floor.

The referee's whistle is shrill. Keep your surroundings as normal as possible. It might be in disarray but it's still the same room. When you come to remember a different list, the journey itself will still be the same – familiar and reliable.

STAGE 7:

   Someone has left a ladder leaning against my front door. I can't avoid knocking it over.

My front door is not a room, but it is another stage on the route. I try to gauge my reaction and timing. How quickly do I grab the rungs, or do I jump out of the way? I hear the clatter of the metal as it crashes to the ground.

STAGE 8:

   A large grandfather clock is ticking away in my front garden, its hands whizzing round backwards.

I am now outside. What is the weather like? Is it raining? If so, it will damage the clock. I walk up to it, round it, see my face reflected in the glass. What time is it? I've never heard such loud ticking.

STAGE 9:

A tape measure is stretched out on the road as far as the eye can see.

I press the release mechanism and listen to the shuffle of metal as the tape begins winding back into the spool at an ever increasing rate. I see the end bobbing up and down as it catches against lumps in the road. I am frightened in case it whips past and cuts me.

STAGE 10:

My opposite neighbour has placed a huge, unsightly bowl in his garden.

'Dog' is written in garish red letters around the side. The bowl itself is yellow and is so large that it completely obscures his house. Dog food is spilling over the lip; great clods of jellied meat are landing in the street all around me.

Reviewing the journey

Once you have created the ten images of your own at ten stages around your house (try not to use my images or stages), you are ready to remember the list by walking around the journey, starting with your bedroom. Review each image. Don't try to recall the object word immediately. You will only get into a panic and confirm your worst suspicions about your memory. There is no rush. Put down this book and move calmly and logically from room to room in your mind.

What is happening in your bedroom? You can hear a clicking sound . . . the fishing rod . . . something slimy: a fish. You go to the bathroom, where you shower every morning . . . the shower . . . something yellow oozing out of the head: margarine. And so on.

Trouble shooting

I am confident that you will remember all ten items. If, however, your mind went a complete blank at any stage, it means that the image you created was not sufficiently stimulating. In which case, return to the list and change the scene. Instead of the ladder falling at stage 7, for example, imagine climbing up a very tall ladder and looking down at the tiny front door. It is windy up there; you are swaying around a lot and feeling giddy. The simple rule of thumb is that your brain, much like a computer (only better), can only 'output' what you've 'input'.

Don't forget, you are exercising your imagination in a new way. Like any underused muscle, it is bound to feel a bit stiff for the first few times. With practice, you will find yourself making images and associations at speed and with little effort.

Success

Using a combination of bizarre images and the familiar routine of a well-known journey, you have stimulated your brain to remember ten random items. You have done more than that, though. Inadvertently, you have repeated them in exact order. Not really necessary for a shopping list, but very useful when it comes to remembering a sequence, something we will come to later.

For now, content yourself with the knowledge that you can start at any stage on the list and recall the items before and after it. Take the clock in the garden, for instance; you know the ladder by the door must come before it, and the tape measure in the street after it. The familiar journey has done all the work for you. It has kept everything in its own logical order.

Don't be alarmed or put off by the seemingly elaborate or long-winded nature of the method. With practice, your brain responds more quickly to creating images on request. It can visualize objects in an instant (images that might take a paragraph to describe); you just have to learn how to train and control it. Before long, you will find yourself 'running' around the route, recalling the objects as you go.

There is also no danger that your head will become too cluttered with all these strange images. The next time you want to remember another list, the new images will erase the old ones. It is just like recording on a video tape. The journey, of course, always remains the same.

It is comforting to know that you are merely developing the way in which the brain already works, rather than teaching it a new method. It is generally accepted that we remember things by association. If you are walking down the street and see a car covered in flowers and ribbons, for example, an image of your own wedding might flash across your brain. This, in turn, reminds you of your husband or wife, and you recall, with horror, that it is your anniversary tomorrow and you haven't done anything about it.

I will now show you an easy way to reinforce these associative images. I know this all seems strange to begin with, but remember: your memory is limited only by your imagination.

A NOTE ON 'LINKING'

I have shown you how to remember ten items on a shopping list by placing them along a familiar journey. Using image, colour, smell, feeling, emotion, taste, and movement, you were able to recall the wilder fruits of your imagination and, in turn, the relevant, mundane item.

This method is adequate for remembering a simple list; sometimes, however, further reinforcement of the images is required, which is where the 'link method' can be used. At each stage on the journey, try giving yourself a taste of what is to follow.

For example, on our original shopping list, the first item was fish; the second, margarine. I remembered the fish by imagining one flapping around at my feet, hooked on to the end of my line. This time, I imagine the fish basted in margarine because I am about to cook it. Or perhaps it flaps its way over to the bedroom door, where a thick yellow liquid is seeping under the door.

The linked image should merely serve as a reminder

of the next item on the list. Be careful not to confuse the two items. The focal point remains the fish and the bedroom.

At stage 2 of the journey, the bathroom, I imagine margarine dripping from the showerhead. This time, using the link method, I see the vague image of chess pieces moving around through the steamed-up glass door. And so on.

Try to make similar links for the rest of the list. The clock hands could be a couple of rulers; the tape measure might be a dog lead. As it begins to recoil, a large dog comes bounding up the road.

Once you feel confident about linking ten simple items, you will be able to extend your journeys and the number of things you can memorize. When I remember a pack of cards, for example, I use a journey with fifty-two stages rather than ten. Sounds daunting? As long as you choose a journey you are familiar with, nothing could be easier.

CHAPTER 3

. . . .

What's in a name?

What's in a name? That which we call a rose
By any other name would smell as sweet.
ROMEO AND JULIET, WILLIAM SHAKESPEARE

NAMES AND FACES

Shakespeare might have been right about roses, but we all know how embarrassing it can be to forget someone's name. People are flattered when you remember it, but insulted when you don't. You might as well tell them, 'You have made no impression on me at all. You don't exist in my world. You are completely forgettable.'

I speak from painful experience. For the first thirty years of my life, I forgot people's names with spectacular enthusiasm. In the early days, I used to wade in with clumsy approximations, near misses that still make me squirm today. Then I switched tactics and started to call people 'there'. 'Hello, there,' I would say, smiling weakly, as old friends came up to me at parties. Worse still, they would invariably ask me to introduce them to people I had only just met.

Mercifully I no longer fear introductions.

Remembering people's names is such a simple skill, and yet it has changed my life. It could change yours if you are prepared to practise a little. I am more confident in social situations, at parties, at business meetings. It has even made me wealthier, or at least it should have done . . .

I was once asked to recall everyone's name at a dinner party in Mayfair, London. The hostess wanted me to memorize the first names and surnames of all her guests, the majority of whom I had never set eyes on before. There were just over a hundred people in total, and they were seated at various tables around the room.

A wealthy businessman sitting on my right didn't believe that this was possible. He had never met me before, but he had heard that I was a professional card-counter – someone who wins at blackjack by relying on mathematics rather than luck. Laughing at the prospect of memorizing over one hundred names, he offered to stake me £50,000 to play the blackjack tables in Las Vegas if I could pull off the stunt.

As far as I was concerned, it was a one-way bet. I agreed to the hostess's wishes and moved from table to table, discreetly asking one person from each to furnish me with names. Using the method you are about to learn, I absorbed all the guests' names before they had even finished their hors-d'oeuvres. I returned to my table. 'Got all the names, have you?' the businessman chuckled nervously. He then suggested that if I was so confident, I should start recalling the names at once, in case I forgot them.

I told him I was hungry and would prefer to eat my dinner first. Besides, there was no hurry. I knew that all the names and faces had been stored in my long-term memory.

As the coffee circulated, I stood up and duly went round the room naming everyone, without making an error, much to the amazement of the guests, not least the businessman. He graciously accepted 'defeat', but we have yet to set a date for Las Vegas. The secret to how I did this is very simple: first impressions.

First impressions

I know exactly what my problem was with remembering names, and I suspect it is the same as yours. Ever since I was a child, I have been bothered by the old adage, 'Never judge a book by its cover.' How many times have you heard it said, 'Don't pigeon-hole people.' 'Don't go on first impressions.'

If you never want to forget someone's name again, I am afraid you must do exactly the opposite: 'Pigeon-hole people!' 'First impressions count!' 'Judge a book by its cover!'

Face the facts

Humans are extremely good at recognizing images they have seen only once. In 1967, the psychologist Shepherd showed a group of people 600 individual slides of pictures, words, and images. He then showed them 68 pairs of slides; one from each pair was from the previous set, and one was new. His subjects were asked to detect the old item. Shepherd recorded an 88 per cent success rate for sentences, 90 per cent for words, and 98 per cent for pictures.

The human face is essentially an image, but psychologists now believe that the brain processes faces quite differently from other images. The existence of prosopagnosia would seem to support this. Prosopagnosia is a rare neurological condition that renders the victims unable to recognize previously familiar faces. Tests have shown that we have difficulty recognizing pictures of faces if they are upside down (Yin, 1969). Inverted buildings, by contrast, present no such problem.

In 1974, Bower and Karlin found that if subjects were instructed to estimate personal characteristics such as honesty and pleasantness, their subsequent memory recognition was enhanced. Bower and Karlin concluded that faces were processed at a deeper, semantic level.

Consequently, I have never understood advice that urges us to ignore our basic, primitive instincts. When a stranger approaches me, I make an instant, intuitive judgement based on their appearance: do I feel comfortable or uneasy, safe or threatened, warm or guarded, indifferent or enchanted? In short, are they friend or foe? An automatic classification process takes place. I then build on that initial reaction to remember the name.

THE METHOD

Now that you have been warned that my method is shot through with unethical principles, I can move on to the nitty-gritty details with a clear conscience. I use a variety of techniques, depending on what the person looks like and the circumstances in which I am introduced to them, but they are all dependent on first impressions. As ever, I exercise my imagination (the key to a good memory) and use location, random places this time, rather than a journey.

Technique 1: Looks familiar

Wherever possible, study a person's face before absorbing his or her name. Ask yourself whether the person reminds you of anyone else. Somebody you already know perhaps, a friend, a relative, or a work colleague. Or maybe he or she resembles a public figure, an actor, a pop star, a sportsperson or a politician.

Your reaction must be immediate. It doesn't matter if the likeness is vague. The person must simply serve as a reminder, a trigger. Let your mind wander. Your brain will sift, computer-like, through the thousands of stored facial patterns you have gathered over the years. In a split second, it will present you with the nearest or next-best link to the person standing in front of you.

You are introduced to a person who, for whatever reason, reminds you of John McEnroe. You have already done half the work, even though you have yet to discover his real name.

You must now imagine a location closely connection to John McEnroe. A tennis court is the obvious place. Think of the centre court at Wimbledon, based on either what you have seen on TV or, better still, an actual visit. If you can't do this, visualize a local tennis court, any court that springs to mind!

All this has gone on in your head in a second, at most. Again, like the journey method in Chapter 2, the process will speed up with practice.

Once you have established a location, you are ready to process their name. He introduces himself as David Holmes. Take the surname first. What does it make you think of? Holmes might suggest Sherlock Holmes. Imagine him on the court, peering through his magnifying glass searching for evidence of chalk dust.

Admittedly, I have used an obvious likeness (McEnroe) and name (Holmes) to show you the basic principle. With a little practice, however, your brain will make associations and form the relevant image more quickly. If, for example, he had been called Smith, you might have imagined a blacksmith setting up his furnace right in the middle of centre court.

The technique works because you are creating what your memory thrives on: a chain of associations. These are the links which you have made so far:

Face	Likeness	Location	Name
(McEnroe)	(tennis court)	(Holmes)	

When you come to meet him later in the evening, you will once again think that he looks like John McEnroe. This makes you think of a tennis court. You will then remember the preposterous sight of Sherlock Holmes on his knees with a magnifying glass, and you have got the name: Holmes.

To remember the first name, in this case David, think of a friend or an acquaintance called David.

Introduce them into the tennis-court scene. Perhaps he is sitting in the umpire's chair.

More often than not, you can think of someone you know with the same first name. But if no one called David springs to mind, use a public or literary figure. You might think of David and Goliath. Picture someone small wielding a sling and tennis ball on the court.

It is very important to use as many of your senses as you can when you are picturing the scene: see the brown patches on the well-worn court, feel the atmosphere of the centre court crowd.

What if David Holmes doesn't remind you of John McEnroe? As far as you are concerned, he looks like a well-known politician. You simply apply the same process. The House of Commons would be a suitable location. Imagine Sherlock Holmes at the dispatch box, berating the Prime Minister. Your friend, David, is sitting in the speaker's chair, desperately trying to maintain order.

When you come to meet the person later, his face again reminds you of the politician. Cue the House of Commons, Sherlock Holmes at the dispatch box, David in the chair and you have got the name: David Holmes.

Or perhaps David Holmes reminds you of your uncle. Imagine Sherlock Holmes at your uncle's house, knocking at the door and smoking his pipe. Your uncle invites him in and introduces him to David, your friend.

And so on. You must use the first associations that come into your head. They are the strongest, most obvious ones, and you are more likely to repeat them when it comes to recalling the person's name.

ISN'T THIS TOO LONG-WINDED?

This method is all very well, you say, but by the time I've worked out the link between face, location and name, thought of McEnroe, been off down to Wimbledon and met Sherlock Holmes, the real David Holmes will have moved on through sheer boredom. Speed comes with practice. It took me barely fifteen minutes to remember over one hundred faces. And the brain is naturally very good at creating associative images.

WHY DOES USING LOCATION IN THIS WAY WORK?

What is going on in your head when you are say, 'Oh, her name's on the tip of my tongue'? Your brain is desperately trying to think of the location you are most used to seeing her in, hoping that this will spark off her name. Failing that, you try to recall the last place where you saw her. It is the same when you lose your car keys. 'Whereabouts did I see them?' 'When did I have them on me last?' You are trying to retrace your steps.

Technique 2: Your typical bank manager

What do you do if you are confronted with someone who resembles no one, not even vaguely? If this happens, try to decide what type of person he or she is. Despite what you might have been told, categorize them! Once again, hang on to the first association that comes into your head.

Let's assume that you meet someone who reminds

you of a typical bank manager. Go through exactly the same mental process as before, this time using your local bank as the location. You are then told his name: Patrick McLennan. Take his surname first. What does it make you think of? Assuming you don't know anyone called McLennan, concentrate on the word itself: 'Mac' and 'Lennan'. Imagine your bank manager in a dirty old raincoat, a flasher's mac, exposing himself to John Lennon. This rather distressing scene would take place in the bank itself.

Now the first name. You happen to know someone called Patrick, who travels abroad a lot, so imagine him standing in a very long queue for the Bureau de Change, waiting to change money. Everyone is naturally shocked at the bank manager's appalling behaviour, not least John Lennon.

When you come to meet this person later in the evening, you would, once again, think that he looked like a typical bank manager. The sordid scene would come flooding back in an instant, and you have his name.

The fact that he is called McLennan and not McLennon is not important, unless you have to write his name down; they are pronounced the same. You must always link the image to how the word is pronounced, rather than spelt. (Featherstonehaugh is pronounced 'Fanshaw', for instance; and 'Chumley' is actually spelt Cholmondeley.)

Similarly, it is important to preserve the order when you are splitting up a name into syllables. You know the bank manager is exposing himself *to* John Lennon, so 'Mac' comes before 'Lennan'. It is fairly obvious in this case, but it becomes more tricky with complicated, polysyllabic names.

Clothes are also important when you are using types. If I met a woman in jodhpurs and a puffa jacket, I would immediately think she was a horserider. If I met a man wearing a loud tie and shirt, I would think he was in advertising. In each case, I use the type to trigger off the most obvious setting: horserider, field or stable; advertising executive, the television room; fashion model, a catwalk; estate agent, an office in the high street.

Only *you* know what a typical bank manager, fashion model, accountant, dustman, cleaning lady, journalist, estate agent, or second-hand car salesman looks like. My idea of a librarian might be your idea of a school teacher. Your Arfur Daley might be my copper. The way we categorize people is based on thousands of previous encounters, either in real life, on TV or in books. You are your own best judge. And no matter how morally wrong it might be to go on appearances, it is the best way to remember names.

Technique 3: Here and now

Some people simply don't remind us of anyone, or any type. They are so bland and uninteresting as to be instantly forgettable. When this occurs, you must use your present surroundings as a location.

Let's assume you are holding a party in a restaurant and are introduced to a guest called Jenny Fielding. Her face reminds you of absolutely no one; her clothes are characterless. In this situation, switch immediately to her name and your present surroundings. 'Fielding' makes you think of a cricket fielder. You happen to know someone else called Jenny, so imagine your friend Jenny dressed in full cricket regalia with her hands cupped, poised to catch a cricket ball in the corner of the restaurant.

What happens if you don't know of anyone named Jenny? You must make one further mental link. Imagine, for example, a donkey (a jenny is a female donkey) acting as a cricket fielder (but don't tell your guest!), or even place an electric generator (genny) at silly mid-off, over by the door. As ever, the more bizarre the image, the more memorable.

Later on, when you are talking with her and a friend of yours approaches, wanting to be introduced, you will think the following:

You are once again reminded of how bland and unlike anyone else this woman is. In such circumstances, you know there must be a link in the present location. Throwing the briefest of glances around the restaurant, you recall the cricket match you had imagined earlier . . . there is the donkey again, shying away from a fierce cover drive. A donkey fielding reminds you of . . . 'This is Jenny Fielding. Jenny, this is my old friend . . .'

Daft, I know, but it works.

Technique 4: Too late

Sometimes you might be given a person's name before you have had time to study their face.

'You must come and meet Victoria Sharpe,' says your boss at the office party, 'I am sure you will like her.' Dragging you by the arm, he takes you over to her. She is a very important person in the company hierarchy and you have only just joined. What do you do?

If I were in this situation, knowing that I had to remember her name, I would think the following, all of which I am imagining now as I write:

Victoria: reminds me of The Victoria Falls. Sharpe . . . razor sharpe . . . someone in a canoe using an enormous razor blade as a paddle, literally cutting through the water.

The moment my boss introduces us, I simply imagine her in the canoe, teetering on the edge of the falls.

Let me give you another example. I was once rehearsing for a TV show (ITV's *You Bet!*) and was told that I would be accompanied by a professional croupier named Jan Towers. Before I had even seen her, I couldn't help thinking of the Tower of London covered in a thick coating of strawberry jam ('Jan'). As soon as we were introduced, I imagined her dealing out hands of blackjack inside the Tower of London using a very sticky deck of cards.

All you are doing when the name comes before the face is reversing the earlier chain of associations and missing out the look-alike stage.

Name	Location	Face

Although I was putting the cart before the horse, the

woman was indelibly linked to her name, thanks to the Tower of London setting. She still is to this day.

Technique 5: Features

Sometimes there is a very obvious link between a person's physical appearance and his or her name. In such cases, there is no point in ignoring it. The 'feature link' technique, as I call it, is a favourite with 'memory men' for shows and party tricks and can work very effectively.

If, for example, you are introduced to a Mr White-head and he appears to be greying above the ears, you imagine someone pouring a pot of white paint over his head. A Mrs Baker comes up and introduces herself. You notice immediately that she has her hair tied in a bun, so you make the obvious connection.

These are obvious examples, I know, but as far as I am concerned, this is the only time when the technique should be used. There has to be a glaring connection between name and appearance.

What you are effectively doing is using the subject's face as a location in which to place their name. But the features can start to overlap after a while, and the technique requires obvious names. Besides, why limit yourself to such a small map as the face, when you can let your imagination remind you of a whole village, a country, or even another part of the galaxy . . .

During a recent show, somebody called Paul Mitchell asked me how I remembered his name. I told him I could imagine a friend of mine called Paul trying delicately to pick up a fragile shell ('-chell') wearing a thick glove ('Mit-') on board the USS *Starship Enterprise*. 'Why *Star Trek*?' he asked. I told him it was because he reminded me of Mr Spock. (I was using technique 1, first impressions. Look-alike: Spock; location: *Starship Enterprise*; name: Mit-chell; first name: my friend Paul.)

The look on his face taught me that you should never fully disclose the details of your mental associations. As it happened, Paul Mitchell reminded me of Mr Spock's manner, rather than his aural attributes. Sadly, no amount of convincing was sufficient, and I fear the poor chap ran off to the nearest mirror.

Whichever technique you use, the secret of my method is in that first, split-second reaction to seeing a face. Your brain makes an instinctive association that must be cherished. Grab hold of it – develop it – and let your imagination do the rest.

One last point: take control of the situation when you are being introduced to people. This might sound obvious, but if you arrive at a party and the hostess reels off the names of ten people all at once, stop her. 'Hang on, one at a time, please. And your name was?' Hear the name correctly and get the person to repeat it if necessary. Say it back to the person as well. It might sound a little awkward, but it is not half as bad as forgetting someone's name two minutes later.

HOW TO REMEMBER LISTS OF NAMES

Occasionally, as part of my show, I am asked to memorize a list of people's names. I am not allowed to see the people; all I am given is a seat number in the audience. Surprisingly, this is almost easier than actually seeing their faces. In Chapter 2, I explained how to use a mental journey to memorize a simple shopping list. When I have to remember a list of people, I simply visualize a person at each stage of a journey, as opposed to an item of shopping.

It is quite an impressive trick to pull off at a party, particularly if you know in which seat everyone will be sitting. You simply number the positions logically, and relate them to stages along your journey.

Let's assume you want to remember a list of ten names in order, the first three of which are Michael Woodrow, Gayle Wheeler and Marcus Spiertanski.

Michael Woodrow: Using the journey around your house (see Chapter 2), you imagine waking up to discover your bedroom is flooded and all your possessions are floating around. Your friend Michael is sitting in an old WOODen tea-chest, ROWing gently out of the door.

Gayle Wheeler: A terrific GALE blows open your bathroom window. The wind is so strong that one of the WHEELS from your car flies through the window, narrowingly missing you, and bounces into the bath with a splash.

Marcus Spiertanski: A pop star called Mark is standing in your spare room, waving a United States (US) flag. Suddenly a SPEAR flies through the air and knocks him to the ground. A huge, TANNED SKIER steps forward and puts his foot victoriously on the slain pop star's chest.

You must use your own imagination in any way you

can. Let it take you off in all directions, but remember to preserve the order of syllables in longer names. No name is insurmountable, providing you break it up into its constituent parts.

Once you have done all ten people on your list, simply move around the house, reviewing the journey, recalling the scenes and, hopefully, remembering the names.

CHAPTER 4

. . . .

How to remember numbers

The problem with numbers is that they are cold and unfeeling. Group a list of letters together and you have a word that represents something – an image, an emotion, a person. Throw a few numbers together and you have, well, you have another number.

So many people find numbers awkward, slippery customers. And yet numbers play such an important part in our lives. Numbers are everywhere. Haven't we all wished, at some time or another, that we could remember numbers without writing them down . . .

Imagine you meet a woman (or man) at a party; she gives you her address – street, floor, and flat number – but you don't have a pen to hand. She goes on to tell you her phone number and fixes a time and day to meet again. The next morning you wake up and can't remember one iota of what she told you. (You can, of course, remember her name, having read Chapter 3.)

You wander downstairs, bleary-eyed and depressed, and open your post. The bank has sent a new Personal Identification Number for your cashpoint card. You think twice about writing it down, remembering what happened last time. On your way to work, you are concentrating so hard on remembering the number, you step out into the street without looking and a car knocks you down. Crawling around on your hands and knees, you find your glasses, glare at the car disappearing into the distance and try to remember its number plate.

A medic asks you for your National Health and National Insurance numbers on the way to hospital; a policeman investigating your accident gets hold of the wrong end of the stick and demands your driving licence. Finally, when the hospital authorities conclude that you can only be treated privately, someone asks for your bank account details or, failing that, your credit card number.

Okay, so we don't all live our lives like Mr Bean. And these days, most of us carry around pens, filofaxes, even personal organizers. But there will always be occasions when we are caught out and need to memorize numbers. In the following chapters I will explain how to remember numbers (up to ten digits) and, in particular, telephone numbers.

THE LANGUAGE OF NUMBERS

How can we be expected to remember six million, three hundred and eighty-seven thousand, nine hundred and sixty-four when we can't touch it, throw stones at it, smell it, pick it up, poke fun at it, marvel at its eating habits? It is inscrutable, inanimate, forgettable. To remember a number you have to breathe life into it, make it come alive by giving it a character, literally.

When I look at a number today, I see a person. If it's a long number, I see an entire scenario unfolding. Each number has been translated into a new language that I can understand and remember.

This new language is at the heart of what I have christened the DOMINIC SYSTEM. (If you like acronyms, I have managed to work one out for D.O.M.I.N.I.C.: Decipherment Of Mnemonically Interpreted Numbers Into Characters!) I originally designed it for competitions. Used properly, it eats numbers for breakfast. I can memorize 100 digits in 100 seconds. Telephone numbers are small fry by comparison. (I explain how to crunch 100-digit monsters in Chapter 22.)

The DOMINIC SYSTEM works by stripping numbers down into pairs of digits, each pair representing a person. The formidable 81,269,471, for example, becomes 81 – 26 – 94 – 71, which in turn relates to four people. But before we get on to big numbers, I would like to show you a simple way to remember single digits.

HOW TO REMEMBER A SINGLE DIGIT BY USING NUMBER SHAPES

The number-shape system provides a useful introduction to the whole concept of translating tedious numbers into memorable objects. It works by associating the physical shape of a number with its nearest, everyday look-alike object. Simple association, in other words. A 4, for instance, might remind you of the profile of a sailing boat. A 2 might suggest a swan. I have listed some suggestions below, but you must settle on what is best for you. Don't worry if it is not in my list at all.

0	=	FOOTBALL, wheel, ring, sun, severed head, hat
1	=	TELEGRAPH POLE, pencil, baseball bat, arrow, phallic symbol
2	=	SWAN, snake
3	=	HANDCUFFS, Dolly Parton, workman's backside (aerial views)
4	=	SAILING BOAT, flag, ironing board
5	=	CURTAIN HOOK, seated lawn mower
6	=	ELEPHANT'S TRUNK, croquet mallet, metal detector, golf club
7	=	BOOMERANG, high diving platform, cliff edge, kerbstone
8	=	EGG TIMER, Marilyn Monroe, transparent potato crisp
9	=	BALLOON AND STRING, basketball net, monocle

I repeat, these are only suggestions. First impressions are, as ever, all important. You should choose the first image that enters your head when you see the shape of a number. Most people, when they look at a '1', think of something long, such as a stick, but if all you keep imagining is the profile of a garden fence or a guard standing to attention, so be it. Choose whatever turns you on. Be careful not to let symbols overlap with each other, though, and make sure that each one is unique. If 6 represents a golf club, don't pick a baseball bat as 1.

Once you have familiarized yourself with the ten key images, you can start using them as props to store and recall simple pieces of information, including position, quantity, and lists.

REMEMBERING POSITIONS

Let's assume you wanted to remember that a friend of yours, or maybe one of your children, came second in a swimming competition. Try to imagine him or her being presented with a swan on the medal rostrum. Or perhaps the reason they came third is because they were wearing handcuffs throughout the race.

Similarly, whenever you visit your aunt, you can never remember which flat it is. To remember that it is number 7, imagine that she has taken to hurling boomerangs around her lounge. (She's getting a little eccentric in her old age.)

REMEMBERING QUANTITY

Your boss has asked you to go out and buy eight cases of wine for the office party. On the way, you visualize him sitting at his desk timing you with an egg-timer – typical of the man. Or perhaps your local wine merchant has miraculously turned into Marilyn Monroe. Make a mental note of how out of place she looks, particularly in a sequin dress.

REMEMBERING LISTS

In Chapter 2, I showed you how to remember a list by using a journey. That system is the basis for my whole approach to memory. There is, however, another simple way of remembering a short list of things in order by using number shapes. Applying your ten shapes, link the following people, in sequence, to the corresponding numbers.

1. Boris Yeltsin
2. John Major
3. Elvis Presley
4. Mother Teresa
5. Frank Sinatra
6. Dalai Lama
7. Charlie Chaplin
8. Steven Spielberg
9. Gary Lineker
10. Prince Charles
(use 0 as the 10th position)

If a telegraph pole is your symbol for 1, imagine Yeltsin shinning up it to mend the wires. (Telecommunications aren't all they could be in the former Soviet Union.) Picture John Major feeding swans instead of talking to the press. Elvis Presley is singing a duet with Dolly Parton, and so on, until you get to Prince Charles being beheaded. (You have to be prepared for some gruesome scenes when you are improving your memory. If it helps, there is a precedent; Charles I was executed in 1649.)

Personally, I prefer to use the journey method (I find it more structured), but this is a good way of exercising your imagination and you might find it easier. A word of warning, though: when you get beyond ten items on the list, it becomes a little complicated without a journey.

The number-shape method plays a small but important part in the DOMINIC SYSTEM. When I am breaking down a long number into pairs of digits, I am often left with a single digit at the end. For example, 37485915274 becomes 37 – 48 – 59 – 15 – 27 – 4. I know the last digit represents a sailing boat. In the next chapter, I will show you what the pairs of digits represent, and how to combine them all in one image.

INTRODUCING THE DOMINIC SYSTEM

My fear of revealing this system to you is that you might be the one person who uses it to break my world records. If you do, I hope that you will pay me the courtesy of acknowledging as much at the award ceremony!

As I said earlier, the trouble with numbers is that they have no resonance. There are, of course, notable exceptions like 13, 21, 69, 100. By and large, however, numbers have little significance outside their own world, which is why they are so difficult to remember.

Enter the DOMINIC SYSTEM. It is based on a new language, so you need to learn a new alphabet. But don't worry, it couldn't be simpler. There are only ten letters, which refer to 0, 1, 2, 3, 4, 5, 6, 7, 8, 9. Ascribe a letter to each digit, and you begin to pull numbers out of the mire of anonymity.

The alphabet

0	=	O	5 = E
1	=	A	6 = S
2	=	B	7 = G
3	=	C	8 = H
4	=	D	9 = N

Let me explain how I arrived at the various letters. Zero obviously looks like the letter O. The first, second, third, fourth, and fifth letters of the alphabet are A, B, C, D, E. Why does 6 not translate into F? This is a personal foible of mine. If it troubles you, or you are a stickler for logic, replace S with F. Personally, I prefer S. Six is a very strong S word. It sussurates, and sounds sexy.

The seventh and eighth letters of the alphabet are G and H; although the ninth is I, I have chosen N, because NiNe is a strong N word.

Memorize this alphabet, and don't continue unless you are certain what each digit stands for.

The language

You are now in a position to give two-digit numbers a character by translating them into the new language. Take 20, for example. This translates into BO (2 = B; 0 = O).

Let the letters suggest a person to you, and use the first association that comes into your head. BO might suggest Bo Diddley or Little Bo Peep.

Or take 27, for example. This translates into BG (2 = B; 7 = G). Again, think of the first person who comes to mind. Barry Gibb, perhaps, a member of the BeeGees.

The numbers are coming to life. One moment 20 is 20, 2 x 10 at a stretch; the next, it's a celebrity. There is no doubt in my mind which is the more memorable.

Write down a list of numbers from 20 to 29 and translate them into letters. Then think of the first person they suggest.

Number	Letters	Person?
20	BO	
21	BA	
22	BB	
23	BC	

24	BD
25	BE
26	BS
27	BG
28	BH
29	BN

Personally, BB suggests a baby; BC makes me think of Jesus Christ; BS reminds me of a BuS driver, BE a BEE-keeper friend of mine.

Every time you look at that number again, you want to think of the same person.

Actions

Staying, for the moment, with these ten numbers (20 to 29), you must now ascribe a unique action to each person. BN (29), for example, makes me think of Barry Norman. His action would be operating a projector. The bus driver's action would be driving a red double-decker. Each action should involve a prop of some sort. If the action is playing the piano, the prop is the piano. If it's skiing, the prop is a pair of skis.

The action should also be as versatile as possible. Later on, when you are memorizing longer numbers, actions and persons are going to fit together like pieces of a jigsaw. It's possible to imagine Barry Norman driving a bus, for example; the bus driver can operate a film projector; an image of him could even be projected.

If the person does not have an obvious action peculiar to him or her, you must discard that person. The importance of actions will become apparent later. Suffice it to say, they make life very easy when you are memorizing more than two digits – telephone numbers, for example.

Once you have drawn up a list of ten persons and actions, start assigning characters to every number from 00 to 99. I suggest doing ten to twenty numbers a day. Each action must be unique, so don't have more than one barmaid, or golfer, or tennis player, or guitarist, and so on.

Auditioning the cast

For the system to work most efficiently, your cast of characters should include a healthy mixture of public and personal names. Don't dwell on the letters themselves; they are simply an intermediary, a way of getting to a memorable image. And try not to ponder on why letters suggest particular people to you. It doesn't matter if your associations are strange, silly or even downright obscene.

Here is a sample of my cast of characters:

01 is my mother, the first person I came into contact with.

My family initials are OB, so 02 (OB) is my father.

19 (AN) reminds me Princess ANne.

When I see 28 (BH), I think of someone I know who spends all their time in the BatH.

60 (SO) makes me think of an old seamstress I know (SO . . . Sewing).

79 (GN) reminds me of a friend called GordoN.

80 (HO) makes me think of Santa Claus – Ho! Ho!

HG is the symbol for mercury, so I associate 87 with a scientist I know.

I have a friend who has a very prominent NoSe; he has become irrevocably linked with 96 (NS).

Memorable numbers

Certain numbers won't need to be translated into letters because they already suggest someone. For instance, 07 makes me think of James Bond; 10 makes me think of Dudley Moore (star of the film *10*). It doesn't matter how you arrive at a person, providing you are sure to make the same association every time.

Initials

You can probably think of around fifty people using the methods I have outlined above. Personally, I managed to come up with about forty-five immediate associations. I then had to start scratching around for the more difficult numbers.

If you are having problems with a number, treat the letters as the initials of a person. Take 33, for example; using the alphabet, this now represents CC (3= C; 3 = C). Or 65, for example: this now translates as SE (6 = S; 5 = E).

Who do you know with the initials CC? Charlie Chaplin, perhaps, or Chubby Checker? or a family friend? What about SE? Stefan Edberg? Sue Ellen?

Write down a list of all those numbers and letters that fail to trigger off any immediate association. Study the letters. Who has the initials BG (27)? Bob Geldof?

45

Boy George? Billy Graham? What about BB (22)? Benazir Bhutto? Boris Becker? Brigitte Bardot?

If you still can't think of someone using the numbers as initials, refer to the following list, *but use it only after you have written out as many numbers as you can. Your associations are the most important.*

NUMBER	LETTER	PERSON	ACTION
00	OO	Olive Oyl	Eating spinach
01	OA	Ossie Ardiles	Playing football
02	OB	Otto (von) Bismarck	Standing on board ship
03	OC	Oliver Cromwell	Loading musket
04	OD	Otto Dix	Painting
05	OE	Old Etonian	Wearing boater
06	OS	Omar Sharif	Playing bridge
07	OG	Organ Grinder	Holding monkey
08	OH	Oliver Hardy	Swinging plank of wood
09	ON	Oliver North	Swearing on oath
10	AO	Aristotle Onassis	Carrying oil can
11	AA	Arthur Askey	Dancing with bees
12	AB	Alastair Burnet	Reading news
13	AC	Andy Capp	Lighting cigarette
14	AD	Arthur Daley	Selling second-hand car
15	AE	Albert Einstein	Chalking a blackboard
16	AS	Arthur Scargill	Carrying sack of coal
17	AG	Alec Guinness	Drinking Guinness
18	AH	Adolf Hitler	Goose-stepping
19	AN	Andrew Neil	Reading newspaper
20	BO	Bill Oddie	Holding binoculars
21	BA	Bryan Adams	Shooting arrow
22	BB	Betty Boothroyd	Banging, order!
23	BC	Bill Clinton	Waving US flag
24	BD	Bernard Davey	Pointing at weather map
25	BE	Brian Epstein	Playing records
26	BS	Bram Stoker	Driving stake in
27	BG	Bob Geldof	Being knighted
28	BH	Benny Hill	Driving milk float
29	BN	Barry Norman	Operating film projector

30	CO	Captain Oates	Building snowman
31	CA	Charles Atlas	Weight-lifting
32	CB	Cilla Black	Blindfolded
33	CC	Charlie Chaplin	Bending cane
34	CD	Christopher Dean	Ice skating
35	CE	Clint Eastwood	Lassooing
36	CS	Claudia Schieffer	Striding along catwalk
37	CG	Charles de Gaulle	Cycling with onions
38	CH	Charlton Heston	Baptizing
39	CN	Christie Nolan	Writing
40	DO	Dominic O'Brien	Playing cards
41	DA	David Attenborough	Crawling in bush
42	DB	David Bowie	Putting on make-up
43	DC	David Copperfield	Performing magic
44	DD	Dickie Davies	Combing hair
45	DE	Duke Ellington	Playing piano
46	DS	Delia Smith	Cooking
47	DG	David Gower	Playing cricket
48	DH	Daryl Hannah	Turning into mermaid
49	DN	David Niven	Percolating coffee
50	EO	Eeyore	Chewing thistles
51	EA	Eamon Andrews	Presenting red book
52	EB	Eric Bristow	Throwing darts
53	EC	Eric Clapton	Playing guitar
54	ED	Eliza Doolittle	Selling flowers
55	EE	Eddie 'The Eagle' Edwards	Skiing
56	ES	Ebeneezer Scrooge	Counting money
57	EG	Elizabeth Goddard	Miming
58	EH	Edward Heath	Conducting
59	EN	Emperor Nero	Giving the thumbs down
60	SO	Steve Ovett	Running
61	SA	Susan Anton	Diving into water
62	SB	Seve Ballesteros	Playing golf
63	SC	Sean Connery	Holding gun
64	SD	Sharron Davies	Swimming with rubber ring
65	SE	Stefan Edberg	Playing tennis
66	SS	Steven Spielberg	Pointing with ET
67	SG	Stéphane Grappelli	Playing violin
68	SH	Sherlock Holmes	Smoking pipe, magnifying glass
69	SN	Steve Nallon	Wearing blue dress

70	GO	George Orwell	In rat cage
71	GA	Gary Armstrong	Passing a rugby ball
72	GB	George Bush	Fishing
73	GC	Gerry Cottle	Swinging on trapeze
74	GD	Gerard Depardieu	Wielding sword
75	GE	Gloria Estefan	Singing
76	GS	Graeme Souness	Operating table
77	GG	Germaine Greer	Burning bra
78	GH	Gloria Hunniford	Interviewing
79	GN	Gamal Nasser	Riding camel
80	HO	Hazel O'Connor	Breaking glass
81	HA	Howard Aiken	Operating computer
82	HB	Humphrey Bogart	Wearing mac and homburg
83	HC	Henry Cooper	Splashing aftershave
84	HD	Humphrey Davy	Holding 'Davy' lamp
85	HE	Harry Enfield	Wearing diamond sweater
86	HS	Harry Secombe	Weighing himself
87	HG	Hughie Green	Knocking on door
88	HH	Hulk Hogan	Wrestling
89	HN	Horatio Nelson	Manning the helm
90	NO	Nick Owen	Sitting on sofa
91	NA	Neil Armstrong	Wearing spacesuit
92	NB	Nigel Benn	Boxing
93	NC	Nadia Comaneci	Balancing on beam
94	ND	Neil Diamond	Sitting on rocks
95	NE	Noel Edmonds	Covered in gunge
96	NS	Nigel Short	Playing chess
97	NG	Nell Gwyn	Selling fruit
98	NH	Nigel Havers	Leading black horse
99	NN	Nanette Newman	Washing up

Power to the people

You should now have a complete list of people from 00 to 99, each one with their own individual action. I have cheated a little. One number reminds me of my late dog (47, DG). You might want to include a pet or a favourite race horse (Desert Orchid works well), but I strongly recommend that you limit yourself to the one animal. Stick with people.

When I was experimenting with this system, I found that certain numbers were far more difficult to remember than others. Those that I had represented by intangible feelings such as love, peacefulness, and anger barely triggered off an image. Certain objects were good stimulants, but people proved to be the best all-rounders.

Committing all these characters to memory might sound like hard work, but it isn't, providing your associations are obvious. With a bit of practice, you will automatically think of two-digit numbers as people; if you can't remember the person, simply refer back to the alphabet (which is why you must learn the ten basic letters before moving on to the people). The letters are there to act as a mental prop. I suggest trying to remember twenty people a day.

HOW TO APPLY THE DOMINIC SYSTEM

Once you have memorized the cast, you have finished the hardest part of this book. They are the key to remembering telephone numbers, credit cards, addresses, any number you want. They even hold the key to memorizing the entire twentieth-century calendar.

How to memorize two-digit numbers

Let's assume that you want to memorize the number of somebody's house. A friend of yours lives at number 74, but you are always knocking at 64 and 84.

Translated into letters, 74 becomes GD, the French actor Gerard Depardieu. Imagine him sticking his sword through the letter box of your friend's house. (In all these examples, I am using well-known people from the list.)

Location is important. Always picture your person at the house you want to remember. You must also ensure that he or she is doing their appropriate action. This helps to link them to their location.

Let's assume another friend of yours lives at number 79; 79 becomes the Egyptian ex-president Gamal Nasser (7 = G; 9 = N). Imagine him tying his camel up outside your friend's house.

Perhaps you want to remember the time trains leave your local station. If it is 8 minutes past the hour, imagine Oliver Hardy (0 = O, 8 = H) standing on the platform, turning around with a plank on his shoulder, sending passengers flying in all directions.

How to memorize three-digit numbers

You are already equipped to remember three-digit numbers. All you have to do is break the number down into a pair of digits and a single digit. For example, 644 becomes 64 – 4. Translate the pair into a person: Sharron Davies (6 = S; 4 = D). And the single digit into a number shape: sailing boat (4). Combine the two and you have an image of Sharron Davies swimming alongside a sailing boat, trying to keep up. Now place this at a relevant location.

If you want to remember the number of a bus, the 295 for example, break it down into 29 – 5. This gives you an image of Barry Norman and a curtain hook. I would imagine him drawing curtains in a bus (parked at the bus stop) and showing a film.

How to memorize telephone numbers

Most telephone numbers in Britain now comprise ten digits. You have already learnt how to memorize two digits by creating an image of one person. It follows that if you want to remember four digits, you have to visualize two people.

But this would only make life half as easy. To memorize someone's telephone number, for example, you would have to visualize five people. Far too much like hard work!

I have stressed throughout this chapter how important it is to give each person an action: Eddie 'The Eagle' is always skiing; Stéphane Grappelli is never without his violin. Actions are the key to remembering any number over three digits; they halve the amount of work you have to do.

Four, six, and eight digits

When you see the number 2914, the first stage is to break it down into 29 – 14, which translates into Barry Norman, and Arthur Daley. But there is no need to visualize them both. Use the first two digits to give you a person, the second two digits to give you an action.

Then combine them to create one image of Barry Norman selling second-hand cars. Arthur is nowhere to be seen. You are interested only in his action, which is selling cars.

29	14
Barry Norman	selling cars
(person	action)

Similarly, if the number were 1429, you would visualize Arthur operating a film camera. Barry Norman would be out of shot completely. His spirit lives on, though, in the action of filming.

The first two digits always refer to the person, the second two digits to an action.

14	29
Arthur Daley	filming
(person	action)

All you are doing is alternating between person and action to create a complex image.

Complex images

Complex images are an efficient way to memorize longer numbers; they condense them into a manageable size. If you have to remember a six-digit number, 142968 for example, break it down into 14 – 29 – 68, and then visualize Arthur Daley filming Sherlock Holmes (68 = SH = Sherlock Holmes). I am simply continuing the process of alternating between person and action.

14	29	68
Arthur Daley	filming	Sherlock Holmes
person	action	person

Taking the example a stage further, let's suppose you have to memorize 14296896. Break it down into 14 – 29

– 68 – 96. Then imagine Arthur Daley filming Sherlock Holmes playing chess (96 = NS = Nigel Short, the chess player).

14	29	68	96
Arthur Daley	filming	Sherlock Holmes	playing chess
person	action	person	action

Five, seven, and nine digits

These numbers work in exactly the same way, except that you have to incorporate a number shape into your complex image to remind you of the single digit. Take 14296, for example. Break this down into 14 – 29 – 6. Then imagine Arthur Daley filming an elephant.

14	29	6
Arthur Daley	filming	elephant's trunk
person	action	number shape

Telephone numbers

We now come to phone numbers themselves. Take the phone number 0122 524593, an ordinary ten-digit number. Apply exactly the same principles as before.

The first stage is to break this number down into pairs of digits: 01 – 22 – 52 – 45 – 93. And then translate them into letters: OA – BB – EB – DE – NC. We are then reminded of five images of people and their actions:

Ossie Ardiles (playing football)
Betty Boothroyd (banging, order!)
Eric Bristow (playing darts)
Duke Ellington (playing piano)
Nadia Comaneci (balancing on a beam)

We combine these people, alternating between person and action, to give us one complex image:

Ossie Ardiles is banging and shouting 'Order!' at an unamused Eric Bristow, who is playing the piano, accompanying one of Nadia Comaneci's delicate routines.

Location is, as ever, essential when remembering phone numbers. It is no good memorizing the number in isolation. It belongs to someone and we must connect the above image to that person. In most cases, the simplest way of doing this is by setting the scene at the house or office of the person whose number we are trying to recall. I remember the number of the person who delivers our logs, for example, by setting the corresponding scene outside his house.

Or take the phone number 0606 922755. Broken down into pairs, the number translates into the following letters: OS – OS – NB – BG – EE.

Omar Sharif (playing bridge)
Omar Sharif (playing bridge)
Nigel Benn (boxing)
Bob Geldof (being knighted)
Eddie 'The Eagle' Edwards (skiing)

We combine these to form a complex image at a relevant location, alternating between person and action:

Omar Sharif playing bridge with Nigel Benn, who is

being knighted by Eddie 'The Eagle' Edwards.

I have outlined the process in detail. With practice, however, you will automatically see images of persons and actions when confronted with a number. I do it automatically now. Life becomes so much easier when you don't have to write down things such as phone numbers.

CHAPTER 5

. . . .

The mental diary

The easiest way to honour appointments is by writing them down in a diary, but there will always be occasions when you have left it behind, or it is not practical to carry one around with you. Large yearly planners can be particularly cumbersome, and even the latest in electronic personal organizers can occasionally go on the blink.

In this chapter, I want to introduce you to an alternative way of remembering appointments: the mental diary. Sadly, our dependence on wall planners, desk charts, and pocket diaries has resulted in a steady decline in our ability to commit dates and meetings to memory. And as I have said all along, if you don't exercise the brain like a muscle, it grows weak. The Japanese, despite their fondness for electronic gadgetry, tend to rely on their memories, and many of them do away with diaries altogether. Remember, the more you exercise the brain, the fitter it becomes.

REMEMBERING APPOINTMENTS

The attraction of flashy year planners is that you can tell at a glance what lies ahead. The forthcoming two months are usually a maze of colour-coded dots, thinning out intoone or two important fixtures later on in the year.

A mental diary works on the same principle. By using a journey with thirty-one stages, you can also tell, at a glance, what treats lie in store. And if you want to look forward to the following month, simply add another route.

THE METHOD

Each stage of the journey represents a day of the month, and appointments are placed at the corresponding stages. Let's suppose you have an appointment with the doctors on 3 January, for example. You simply go to the third stage, where your appointment is represented by a key image. Imagine your doctor standing there in a white coat, for example, with a stethoscope around his or her neck.

THE JOURNEY

On top of a hill in Surrey, there is an old brick folly. As a young boy, I used to climb up its precarious steps, ignoring all thoughts of my own safety, and stand proudly on the top. From there I had a good view of two villages below me. To the east lay the village of Wonersh, to the west, Bramley. It was the perfect lookout post. I could clearly make out individual roads, rivers, and people in both villages.

Today, I use this panoramic setting for all my appointments. The journey from the tower to Bramley covers all my engagements in the month ahead; the journey to Wonersh is for the second month ahead. Below, I have given you the journey to Bramley, together with a typical month of appointments.

One-month planner

STAGE	JOURNEY TO BRAMLEY	DATE	JANUARY APPOINTMENTS
1	Tower	1	
2	Bushes	2	
3	Well	3	Doctor's
4	Secret tunnel	4	
5	Fence	5	Golf lesson
6	Gardens	6	
7	Driveway	7	Wedding (Steve and Caroline)
8	Stables	8	
9	Stile	9	Board meeting (head office)
10	Steep path	10	Hairdresser's
11	Steps	11	
12	Road	12	Bank manager
13	Bomb shelter	13	
14	Barn	14	
15	River bank	15	Dinner party
16	Bridge (on top)	16	Collect Toby, Heathrow (0900 hours)
17	Jetty	17	Accountant
18	Boat	18	Jane's 40th Birthday (card)
19	Weeping willow	19	Dentist (1100 hours) Golf lesson (1700 hours)
20	Back garden	20	Squash
21	Back door	21	
22	Bridge (under)	22	
23	Cricket pitch	23	School play
24	Pavilion	24	
25	Golf club	25	
26	Bus stop	26	Golf lesson
27	Garage	27	Chiropodist
28	Hotel	28	Car insurance due
29	Mini-roundabout	29	
30	Restaurant	30	
31	Library	31	

Reviewing the diary

If I 'stand' on my folly, I notice immediately that there is considerable activity down by the river. I must have a lot of engagements that week. Similarly, I can see that the beginning of the month is pleasantly quiet – a solitary doctor standing by the well and my golf tutor over by the fence.

The advantage of both routes is that I can see all the stages from the same vantage point, enabling me to spot in an instant the congested areas – busy days or weeks, in other words.

The stages themselves are carefully chosen; it is important to use open spaces and outside features such as bridges, roads, and rivers, from where you can see plenty of days ahead. I have also ensured that the distance between each stage remains constant. This makes it easier to spot congestion.

It's up to you how often you choose to review your diary. I look at mine once a day, first thing each morning. I stand at the relevant stage and survey what lies ahead. As the days pass, I move further along the journey.

Occasionally, I return to my folly for an overview and glance at the whole month. I also keep an eye on Wonersh. The second journey (February) will naturally begin to fill up as the first month comes to an end. I try to add images the moment I fix another appointment. You can't blame your mental diary if you've forgotten to 'write' an appointment down.

Between them, the two journeys cover the whole year, taking alternate months. As February passes, and I make my way towards Wonersh, the journey to

Bramley will start to fill up, this time with March's events. I am using the video again, erasing the old images as I record new ones. As March passes, the journey to Wonersh will fill up with April's appointments. And so on.

If you are extremely busy and need to confirm dates three months ahead, simply use a third route and rotate between the three of them.

How to choose your own journey

My two journeys bring back happy childhood memories of charging around the Surrey countryside, exploring deserted pill boxes, climbing trees, catching fish. If you are going to use a mental diary regularly, it is essential that the journey itself is a pleasant experience. There is little to be gained by throwing yourself into a deep depression every morning.

Remember, too, that your journey must be completely deserted as you map it out in your head; this will ensure that the images stand out clearly when you come to populate the stages. And try to reinforce certain key stages throughout the month, like the 5th, or 11th or 21st; this will help you to find dates more quickly. (My 21st stage involves a door.) The next time someone asks you if you are free on a certain day, you will be able to tell them in an instant, instead of fumbling around and muttering, 'I'll have to check my diary.'

Examples

Here is how I would remember some of the appointments from my imaginary January:

---

5 January: Golf lesson
The location is the 5th stage, which is a fence. The key image is of my tutor chipping golf balls. He is knocking them over the fence.

7 January: Steve and Caroline's wedding
The location is the driveway to a splendid manor house built by Sir Edward Lutyens (7th stage). The key image is of Steve and Caroline. They are making their way down the drive in a wedding carriage, dressed in brilliant white. Confetti is flying everywhere.

9 January: Board Meeting, Head Office
The location is a wooden stile (9th stage). The key image is of my boss. He is trying in vain to conduct a board meeting, and he looks a little silly sitting on the stile.

15 January: Giving a dinner party
The location is the river bank (15th stage). The key image is of my guests sitting around a table. They are on the river bank, waiting impatiently for someone to catch a fish so they can get on with their dinner.

28 January: Insure car
The location is the hotel (28th stage). The key image is of my car, badly crumpled at the front. It has been towed to the hotel car park. This depressing image would shock me into re-insuring it.

How to remember the time of an appointment
The whole purpose of the mental diary is to improve

your awareness of future engagements and plans. There is nothing to stop you from using it in conjunction with a written diary. The sight of a doctor standing by a well, for example, need only be a reminder of the day. You can always then check the time of your appointment in a diary.

Having said that, the mental diary is well equipped to record the time of an appointment. Using the twenty-four-hour clock, you can translate times into people and incorporate them in your image.

If, for example, my board meeting on 9 January was at 1600 hrs, I would imagine Arthur Scargill interrupting the meeting by delivering a sack of coal (16 = AS = Arthur Scargill).

It helps to reinforce the time image if you include the person's action, but it is not always necessary. Here are two more examples:

16 January: Collect Toby from Heathrow at 0900 hrs
The location is the bridge (16th stage). The key image is of Toby. An aeroplane has landed on the bridge and he is disembarking, accompanied by Oliver North (09 = ON = Oliver North).

19 January: Dentist's appointment at 1100 hrs. Golf lesson at 1700 hrs.
The location is the willow tree (19th stage). In this particular example, I have two appointments on the same day, so I imagine two separate key images, one on either side of the willow tree. The first key image is of my dentist. He is drilling a hole in one of Arthur

Askey's teeth (11 = AA = Arthur Askey). The second key image is of my golf tutor. He is teaching Alec Guinness how to stop hooking the ball (17 = AG = Alec Guinness).

Who needs a filofax anyway?

The mental diary has a virtually limitless capacity to store information. All you have to do is translate the data into images and incorporate them in your scene. Let's suppose that I had to collect Toby from Heathrow Terminal 3 on 16 January. I imagine Oliver North wearing handcuffs (number shape for 3) and being escorted by Toby down the steps of the aircraft.

Planning the whole year

I said earlier that if you wanted to plan for more than two months ahead, you should rotate among three separate journeys. However, if you have only the odd event to remember throughout the rest of the year, stick with your two main journeys and use a third, short one, consisting of ten stages.

I have just such a route, heading out north from my tower. If I need to remember an art exhibition on 27 August, for example, I would create an image of the first stage: Bob Geldof swinging a plank of wood around while admiring a painting.

I arrive at this image as follows: the key image is the painting, reminding me that it is an art exhibition. The date is the 27th; 27 = BG = Bob Geldof. August is the 8th month; 08 = OH = Oliver Hardy, whose action is swinging a plank.

The chronological order does not need to be preserved along this shorter journey; the dates are contained within each image. If I am subsequently invited to a farewell barbecue with some friends on 22 June, I move to the second stage and imagine my friends watching Betty Boothroyd playing bridge on the barbecue. (They could have been playing tennis.)

You should know by now how I arrived at this particular scene. The key image is the barbecue. The date is the 22nd; 22 = BB = Betty Boothroyd. June is the 6th month; 06 = OS = Omar Sharif, whose action is playing bridge.

CHAPTER 6

· ·

The mental in-tray

THE LIST DISEASE

In the last chapter, I showed you how to remember appointments, but what about everyday chores and tasks that we never get around to doing? I must cut the grass, you tell yourself; I must do something about the woodworm in the kitchen table; I must drop in on the old lady at the end of the road; I must join the health club. The tasks seem to add up, and you never get around to doing any of them.

It can all become quite stressful. You start to exaggerate the problem – 'I have got so many things I should be doing' – even though you could probably count them on one hand. The answer, of course, is to order your chores by writing them down, which is why we have become a nation of list-writers. But even this practice is not without its stresses. Bits of paper can get lost. Worse still, you can become an obsessive list-maker, buying in truck loads of 'Post-its' and plastering your walls with memoranda. In extreme cases, you draw up the mother of all lists once a morning, detailing the lists that you must write during the day.

THE CURE

Let me suggest a calm and effective alternative: the

mental in-tray. Choose a simple journey with ten stages. It is important that the place holds happy memories for you. I use a hotel I stayed at on a wonderful holiday. Why not use somewhere from your honeymoon (providing it wasn't a disaster)? Or a scene from your childhood?

Once you have established and memorized the ten stages, run through all the chores, tasks, or general worries that are currently troubling you. Then create a key image for each one and place them at separate stages. Here is a typical in-tray:

The mental in-tray

CHORE	KEY IMAGE	ROUTE
1. Extend overdraft	Bank manager	Sunny beach
2. Bathroom leak	Plumber	Bar
3. Cut grass	Lawnmower	Restaurant
4. Stop smoking	Dirty ash tray	Hotel drive
5. Letter to relative	Aunt in tears	Reception
6. Pay phone bill	Superman/phone box	Lounge
7. MOT	Car	Pool
8. Shopping	Supermarket trolley	Bedroom
9. Develop photos	Camera	Jacuzzi
10. Hoover house	Vacuum cleaner	Balcony

The bizarre image of a supermarket trolley tucked up in bed can mean only one thing: my turn to do the shopping. And the sight of my aunt in tears, pouring her heart out to the somewhat bemused hotel receptionist, is a sharp reminder that a letter is well overdue.

Priority is not important. Once all your worries are out in the open and pleasant surroundings of your journey, you will have an equal awareness of each of them, allowing you to get them into some sort of perspective.

OTHER USES

A mental in-tray has many other uses. I find it invaluable when I am attending a meeting, or conducting an important phone conversation. If there are certain key points which I want to convey, I translate them into images and put them along my in-tray journey. Nothing is more frustrating than the sudden realization, usually on the bus home, that you have forgotten to say your most important point at a crucial meeting.

I also use it last thing at night. If I must leave a note for the milkman, I imagine a bottle of milk at stage 1. Similarly, if I ever have to go on a course of pills, taking three a day, for example, I move an image of a bottle to the next stage every time I take a dose. Perhaps its most useful application, though, is in a job interview.

CHAPTER 7

. . . .

Memory and job interviews

Before I became a full-time Memory Man, I once applied for a job at an airport. Sensing that I had to pull something special out of the hat if I were to get it, I decided to swot up on some background information. I memorized every piece of data I could find about the company, and I also learnt all I could about each airline that operated out of the airport.

The interview went well. I tried to give the impression that I was genuinely interested in the overall environment. It must have paid off because I landed the job. Thanks to a trained memory, I was referring to a mental in-tray throughout the interview, reminding myself of salient points which I thought should be raised. I had also used an extended journey to file away the information about the company and airlines.

In today's difficult employment market, interviews are more important than ever; a trained memory can help you to make the most of them. Think how refreshing it is for an interviewer to be sitting opposite an applicant who has bothered to find out about the firm beforehand. Not only that, but the applicant comes across as intelligent, recalling detailed and relevant information seemingly at will. When asked about his or her CV, the reply is clear and concise, with no 'umming' and 'erring' or 'I can't remember what I was doing then'. And finally, when the interviewer asks if there are any questions, the applicant raises considered, well thought-out queries.

THE IN-TRAY

The chief purpose of using a mental in-tray for a job interview is to order your thoughts, allowing you to ask all the questions you wanted to before walking in through the door. There's nothing worse than planning what you are going to say, perhaps even scribbling something down on a scrap of paper in the waiting room, and then cursing yourself afterwards, 'I wish I'd asked this; I completely forgot about that.' The tense atmosphere of an interview can ruin your composure and clarity of thought unless you have a strong mental structure to hold everything together.

In-trays for interviews are created in exactly the same way as I described in the previous chapter: keep the journey short and simple (no more than ten stages), and use instant association to create your key images. The only difference is that you might want to place your questions in order of priority. As the conversation progresses, walk along your short journey letting the key images trigger off the questions.

I find that an in-tray and a longer journey work very well in tandem. A question about a certain aspect of the company's operations, for example, might be the cue for calling up a separate journey containing all the relevant data on that subject.

Journeys

There is no limit to the information that can be stored using journeys: facts and figures about the company, including balance sheets and its history; information relating to customers, branches, key employees; data about the general sector of industry; related share prices.

But be careful! Don't show off too much; you may unnerve your interviewer if you suddenly reel off the company's entire annual accounts. The odd subtle throwaway line at the right moment is far more likely to leave the right lasting impression.

When you are choosing a journey, exactly the same principles apply as before. Try to ensure that it has some relevance. The first stage could start at the firm itself, perhaps. If you have come to know your Job Centre well over the last few weeks and months, it could always begin there.

Always keep the data as visual as possible. No matter how technical or involved the information might be, there is always a way of translating it into key images. Use all the techniques you have learnt: the DOMINIC SYSTEM for converting statistics into people and actions, word association to remember important members of staff.

Finally, you may wish to use a separate journey for your career. There's nothing worse than being asked about a dark and distant period in your previous employment and not being able to shed any light on it.

Break down your CV into its constituent parts, and translate them into key images. Again, the DOMINIC SYSTEM can be used to make dates more memorable; alternatively, you could assign each year to a separate stage.

No matter how well prepared you are, or how much research you have done, you won't get the job if you don't perform well in the interview. Mental composure is essential. A good memory allows you to maintain your train of thought in the often difficult environment of an interview, bringing out the best in you when it matters.

CHAPTER 8

. . . .

How to remember speeches

This chapter is for public speakers. You might be a barrister, lawyer, politician, comedian, priest, lecturer, actor, or perhaps you've been asked to make a speech at a wedding or after dinner. We all have to address others in public at some time in our lives, and for many of us it can be a nerve-wracking occasion. A trained memory can help you to deliver a good speech, effortlessly and without any worry.

BAD SPEECHES

A badly prepared speech or talk is not only embarrassing for the speaker, it can also be acutely painful for the audience as well. For those who try to speak without notes, jokes can often fall apart in public, even though they went well in private beforehand. Ideas tend to peter out rapidly when you are ad-libbing, and remembering a punchline is so much more difficult when the pressure is on to perform.

There is also nothing worse than someone reading out an anecdote verbatim from a piece of paper. Their speeches are often punctuated with pregnant pauses as they desperately try to decipher their own handwriting.

72

KEY POINTS

Anyone who has tried to avoid these pitfalls and attended a public speaking course will have probably been told to condense speeches into a series of key points. Listed on a cue card, they are designed to trigger off particular anecdotes, subjects or aspects of a story. They are written out in sequence, thus preserving the natural order of the speech.

This technique usually results in a big improvement, but relying on an external memory aid such as a cue card can still interrupt the flow of a speech. (I am sure you have seen someone nervously shuffling their cards.) The most successful public speakers, however, are able to store their key points in their heads.

Enter the mental speech file. Much like the mental diary, a speech file can help you to remember a talk in its entirety without any notes. Key points are translated into key images, and placed along a simple journey.

The following is a slightly edited version of one of Rowan Atkinson's infamous wedding speech sketches, taken from his *Live in Belfast* recording. If you haven't heard this masterful performance before, imagine him delivering it in a begrudging, acrimonious tone.

Pray silence for the Father of the Bride

Ladies and Gentleman and friends of my *daughter*. There comes a time in every wedding reception when the man who paid for the damn thing is allowed to speak a word or two of his own. And I should like to take this opportunity, sloshed as I may be, to say a word or two about Martin. As far as I'm concerned, my daughter could not have chosen a more delightful, charming, witty, responsible, wealthy – let's not deny it – well placed, good-looking and fertile young man than Martin as her husband. And I therefore ask the question: Why the hell did she marry Gerald instead?

. . . If I may use a gardening simile here: if his entire family may be likened to a compost heap – and I think they can – then Gerald is the biggest weed growing out of it. I think he is the sort of man people emigrate to avoid.

I remember the first time I met Gerald, I said to my wife – she's the lovely woman propping up that horrendous old lush of a mother of his – either this man is suffering from severe brain damage, or the new vacuum cleaner has arrived. As for his family, they are quite simply the most intolerable herd of steaming social animals I've ever had the misfortune of turning my nose up to. I spurn you as I would spurn a rabid dog. I would like to propose a toast . . . to the caterers. And to the pigeon who crapped on the groom's family limousine at the church. As for the rest of you around this table not directly related to me, you can sod off. I wouldn't trust any of you to sit the right way on a lavatory.

(written by Richard Curtis and Rowan Atkinson)

Not many fathers are likely to stand up and deliver a tirade like this, although many would like to, but it is a very good example of what can be achieved using your memory. Timing, emphasis, and rhythm can make all the difference between a faintly amusing speech and a hilarious one. If you have a mental list of key points in your head, you can pace yourself better, knowing what's come up and what you've already said.

A speech file enables you to 'see' the entire contents laid out in front of you (like the mental diary), letting you make a smooth transition from point to point. As you are talking, you can 'walk' down your journey. A key image for each new point will appear in front of you, and those beyond it will also be visible. There's no chance of your rhythm being disrupted, providing, of course, you have chosen a familiar journey and don't lose your way!

THE SPEECH FILE

I have divided the 'Father of the Bride' sketch into twenty-two points to show you how a speech can be converted into key images. You should be able to understand it all from the following.

1.	Daughter	12.	Compost heap
2.	Wallet	13.	Weed
3.	Martin	14.	Passport
4.	Light	15.	Wife
5.	Snake charmer	16.	Gerald's mother
6.	Comedian	17.	Vacuum cleaner
7.	Keys	18.	Herd
8.	Gold bar	19.	Rabid dog
9.	Well	20.	Caterers
10.	Ram	21.	Pigeon
11.	Gerald	22.	Loo

Notice how I have translated into key images the run of

seven adjectives that describe Martin:

delightful	light
charming	snake charmer
witty	comedian
responsible	keys
wealthy	gold bars
well-placed	well
fertile	ram

I have also made 'passport' the key image for 'emigrate'. This works well for me, but you might have a more obvious association. Whenever you are forming key images, you must remember that you have got to make the link again, and in a more pressured situation. I can't stress enough that the first associations are always the most important.

Choose your own journey, and try converting the 'Father of the Bride' speech into key images. (Don't forget that facts and figures can easily be translated into memorable images using the DOMINIC SYSTEM.) Then practise delivering it without writing anything down.

The next time you have to deliver a less vitriolic wedding speech, make sure you use a mental speech file. It looks so much more impressive than scrawny notes or smart cue cards. I suggest you choose a journey that involves a church, and be certain to memorize the route before you start filling it with key images.

A mental speech file is such a simple way of making a big impression. Whether it's a wedding, or an important business presentation, you are bound to be noticed if you calmly stand up, and deliver a polished and appropriate speech with *no real notes*.

CHAPTER 9

. . . .

How to remember directions

If you want to join the ranks of London's 23,000 drivers of black taxis, you first have to pass a gruelling test known as 'the Knowledge'. Among other things, it requires that you learn 468 routes around the capital, including 5,500 roads, and a whole host of museums, churches, hospitals, railway and police stations, theatres, parks, and other landmarks. It's hardly surprising that the success rate for passing is a mere 30 per cent.

In 1992, I was asked by *Auto Express*, a motoring magazine, to memorize four routes from 'the Knowledge'. My examiner was none other than Fred Housego, celebrity cabbie and winner of *Mastermind*. Never one to do things by halves, Fred asked me to sit blindfolded in the back of his cab before driving me around what he considered to be the toughest routes in London. (Anyone who saw us probably thought I was being kidnapped.)

Fred sang out the directions to me as we went along: 'Left into Southwark Street. First into Blackfriars Road. Forward Blackfriars Road. Remember the sandwich shop on the right. Continue into New Bridge

Street. Leave New Bridge Street for Farringdon Street. Spot the station on your right. Turn right at traffic lights into Clerkenwell Road.'

On and on we went, twisting and turning through the streets of London, passed St Paul's, through Covent Garden and Trafalgar Square, around the Houses of Parliament. I wondered if it would ever end. Once the ordeal was over, however, I was able to recite perfectly the instructions for all four routes, including details like the sandwich shop on Blackfriars Road. Even Fred was a little bemused: 'I've never met a cabbie who can do anything like this!' he told the magazine. 'I gave him the hardest routes and he scored 100 per cent.'

It would have only confused the issue if I had disclosed that my mind hadn't been on the streets of London at all. I had, in fact, been taking a leisurely stroll around East Herts golf course.

HOW TO USE A GOLF COURSE FOR REMEMBERING DIRECTIONS

Most of us tend not to be given instructions sitting blindfolded in the back of a black cab. They are usually offered in a hurry, through a wound-down window. Or we are standing in a draughty phone box, lost in the dark and without a pen, desperately trying to remember what the person on the other end of the line is saying.

'Go left at the lights,' they say.

'Right,' you reply.

'Left, not right!'

'Right, I mean left!'

And so on.

If you are ever in this predicament again, try using a familiar journey to record the instructions. And I urge anyone who plays golf to choose a route around their favourite course. It doesn't matter if you're not a player; a country walk or a route through your town will more than suffice.

A round of golf is not such an odd choice for a journey as it might sound. I think it is fair to say that most golfers, on completing a round, are able to recall individual strokes; also the exact spot where the ball landed, their choice of iron or wood, and even their opponent's play. The next time you are in a clubhouse, grit your teeth for a few seconds and listen to the golf bores as they trade descriptions of miraculous second shots on the seventh fairway or twenty-footers at the fifteenth green.

What's going on here? Are people suddenly being imbued with wonderful powers of recall every time they play a round of golf? If you were to ask any club player how he or she approached the third shot on the seventeenth, or how many putts they took on the fourth, they could probably tell you. In fact, they could probably take you through an entire round, recalling 80 to 100 shots in perfect sequence. It's all beginning to sound familiar. Isn't this exactly the sort of memory trick I perform, except with playing cards and numbers rather than golf shots?

So why do we have such a problem remembering eight to ten road directions, when we can recall 80 to 100 golf shots in a trice? If you have understood my approach to memory, you already know the answer. A logical journey around a golf course, with each stage sequentially numbered, is bound to give order to an otherwise ramshackle set of memories. It's exactly the same technique you learnt for memorizing lists and appointments. Even if you're not interested in golf, it is a perfect example of the hidden potential our memories possess.

DIRECTIONS

Imagine you are given the following instructions to remember. You don't have the time or wherewithal to write them down; besides, it's hazardous trying to read and drive at the same time.

1. Left into Western Avenue
2. Right into Cannonsgate Road
3. Third exit off the roundabout
4. T-junction: right into Station Road
5. Pass Red Lion Pub on the left
6. T-junction: left into Braintree Road
7. Straight on for four miles
8. Second set of traffic lights: turn right
9. First exit off roundabout into Warren Way
10. Sixth House on the left: Blacksmith Cottage.

It's a daunting challenge, but you were meant to be at Blacksmith Cottage half an hour ago for an important supper engagement. Let me tell you how I would memorize these instructions, using a golf course as my journey.

I relate each direction or signal to an imaginary strike

of a ball and its subsequent position. Turning left, for instance, is represented by a ghastly hook shot; turning right is a slice; straight on is a satisfying drive plumb down the middle of the fairway; a roundabout is a green; and a T-junction is the next tee. I translate names of roads, pubs and other landmarks into memorable images – exaggerated, colourful, bizarre – which are then incorporated in my round. As I said earlier, I personally imagine myself standing at the first tee at East Herts golf course.

1. Left into Western Avenue
To remember 'left', I imagine driving a wild hook off to the left-hand side of the first fairway (not unusual for me). To remember 'Western Avenue', I picture a hostile, action-packed scene of cowboys and indians engaged in mortal combat on the spot where the ball has landed.

2. Right into Cannonsgate Road
This time I imagine slicing the ball way over to the right-hand side. It's going to be a tricky one to play: the ball has disappeared straight down the shaft of an old cannon that is leaning on a gate.

3. Third exit off the roundabout
Roundabouts are always represented by greens, and I remember the exit by the number of putts it takes to sink the ball. My putting has always let me down and today is no exception: I three putt at the first. Alternatively, I could imagine myself standing handcuffed to the flag. Handcuffs are the number shape for 3.

4. T-junction: right into Station Road

The T-junction automatically takes me to the next tee, where I promptly slice the ball again to the right. Unlike most slices, however, the ball doesn't disappear into thick undergrowth. I imagine it landing on a station platform and bouncing mercilessly through the crowd, scattering terrified commuters in all directions.

5. Pass Red Lion Pub on the left

My next shot lands in a nasty bunker to the left of the green. As I approach, I see a ferocious red lion guarding the ball. He is prowling round and round it, looking distinctly menacing. I think I'll concede the hole.

6. T-junction: left into Braintree Road

At the next tee, it's another hook, I am afraid. The ball skews off to the left of the fairway by a tree – a very thoughtful tree, as it happens. Looking up, I am amazed to see a large brain wedged between two of its branches. The Tree of Knowledge, no less. This will make a fine story back at the clubhouse (zzzzzzzzzzzzzz . . .)

7. Straight on for four miles

At last! My game is coming together. I hit the ball straight down the middle of the fairway with my four iron. (Once again, I could also incorporate a number shape, in this case a yacht, to remember four miles.)

8. Second set of traffic lights: turn right

My next shot lands in the rough on the right. Ahead of me, I imagine a large traffic light, rising out of an inconveniently positioned lake. A swan is swimming round the pole, as if protecting it. A swan is the number shape for 2.

9. First exit off roundabout into Warren Way

My green play is improving: I single putt the next shot. But it's not only the length of the putt that is impressive. The green is crowded with rabbits from a nearby warren. Alternatively, I imagine that the flag has turned into a telegraph pole (the number shape for 1) to remind me that it's the first exit. Not surprisingly, I prefer to putt at roundabouts when it's the first exit.

10. Sixth house on the left: Blacksmith Cottage

Finally, I hit a six iron off to the left of the next fairway, and watch, in disbelief, as it lands in the furnace of a blacksmith who has set up shop on the course. Alternatively, I picture an elephant (number shape for 6) being fitted with a shoe by a blacksmith.

They may be surreal, crazy images, but I bet I arrive at the supper engagement before you do.

CHAPTER 10

. . . .

Learning the twentieth-century calendar

Monday's child is fair of face
Tuesday's child is full of grace
Wednesday's child is full of woe
Thursday's child has far to go
Friday's child is loving and giving
Saturday's child works hard for a living
And the child that is born on the Sabbath day
Is bonny and blithe, and good and gay

On 11 September 1978, a Bulgarian playwright named Georgi Markov was queuing at a bus stop on the Embankment in London. He was on his way to Bush House on the Strand, where he worked as a translator for the BBC's World Service. Shortly before his bus arrived, he felt a sharp jab in the back of his leg. Witnesses said they saw a man walking off in a hurry, carrying an umbrella. Four days later, Markov was dead. The police suspected poisoning.

I was recently reminded of this notorious assassination by a magazine article on the Bulgarian secret police. As I read it, I tried to picture the scene: why was he poisoned at a bus stop? Was there anything relevant about the date? I knew in an instant that Markov was stabbed on a Monday. It was a small point, but it helped to set the scene for me. He was a normal commuter, going to work like the rest of us. But what a tragic start to the week!

I knew it was a Monday because I have 'learnt' the twentieth-century calendar. I could similarly tell you in an instant what day of the week it was on 19 August 1905 (Saturday), or 22 December 1948 (Wednesday); and I know what day it will be on 1 January 1998 (Thursday).

It's an extremely useful skill to acquire, one that I personally use all the time. It's also a very entertaining party trick. As part of my stage show, I ask someone to tell me their date of birth; before they've had time to say, 'It's a con!', I have told them which day of the week they were born on, and which famous people they share their birthdays with. Surprisingly, there is very little to learn; you have already done most of the work in previous chapters.

THE PARTY

Imagine that today is your birthday. As a present, a friend has organized a surprise party for you. You come home from work to find that your house has been taken over by 100 guests, a mixture of friends, relatives, and famous people.

The guest list bears an uncanny resemblance to the people you memorized for the DOMINIC SYSTEM. This time, however, the characters represent years, from 1900 to 1999. Take Benny Hill, for example (or your

equivalent character suggested by BH). Using the
DOMINIC SYSTEM, he represents 1928 (2 = B; 8 = H).
Or Betty Boothroyd, the Speaker of the House of
Commons. She represents 1922 (2 = B; 2 = B).

The house is too small to accommodate all the guests
in one room, so your friend has allocated each person
to a particular room, and told everyone to stay there
for the whole evening. One group has even been
banished to the garden. As far as possible, they have
been spread evenly; some areas have fourteen people
and some fifteen. I will tell you in a moment who has
been allocated where.

THE METHOD

When someone tells me a date, I make an instant and
simple calculation. The date is broken down into its
component parts, year, month, and day, and I give
each one a basic numerical code (anything between 0
and 6). I then add them together to work out the day of
the week. The party scene you have just imagined is an
easy way of remembering the relevant codes.

The year code

The setting for your party should consist of six rooms
and your garden. Each area much be distinct and have
familiar associations: furniture, pictures, windows. It
doesn't have to be your own house. You might prefer
to choose your place of work, a health club, a school,
your parents' home. It is important, however, that you
use the location solely for calculating the twentieth-
century calendar.

Allocate to each room a number between 0 and 6. As the garden is not a room, we will call it zero. I suggest that you use the simplest number-shape method to remember the other numbers.

Area	Number	Shape	Association
Garden	0	Football	Playing in the garden.
Bedroom	1	Telegraph pole	BT have erected an unsightly pole outside your bedroom window.
Spare room	2	Swan	A rather tasteless porcelain swan ornament sits on the dresser (that's why it is in the spare room).
Staircase	3	Handcuffs	I always keep these handy at the top of the stairs in case I have to arrest an unwelcome intruder.
Lounge	4	Sail boat	The seascape oil painting above the fireplace depicts a sailing boat.
Kitchen	5	Curtain hook	Why are the curtains drawn in the kitchen?
Bathroom (downstairs)	6	Elephant's trunk	An elephant's trunk acts as a shower attachment (another tasteless feature, I am afraid).

The next stage is to work out where each person has been allocated. This will give you the all-important code number (between 0 and 6) for the year you have been asked. If someone says they were born in 1972,

87

for example, you need to know that George Bush (GB = 72) is in the bathroom, which gives you the code 6.

Room allocation

Here is a list of the people who have gathered in the garden, and the years they represent. Needless to say, you should use your own characters – a mixture of personal acquaintances and celebrities. For the purposes of demonstration, however, I will use the people on the list in Chapter 4.

Garden: Code number 0 (football)

Olive Oyl 1900	Eamon Andrews 1951
Omar Sharif 1906	Ebeneezer Scrooge 1956
Alec Guinness 1917	Seve Ballesteros 1962
Bill Clinton 1923	Gerry Cottle 1973
Benny Hill 1928	Gamal Nasser 1979
Christopher Dean 1934	Humphrey Davey 1984
Duke Ellington 1945	Nick Owen 1990

Imagine each person in a different part of your garden. Make people interact, and incorporate the actions you gave them in the DOMINIC SYSTEM. Omar Sharif is playing bridge with Ebeneezer Scrooge. Gerry Cottle is swinging on a trapeze at the end of the garden above Benny Hill's milk float. Bill Clinton is being interviewed by Nick Owen, who is sitting on a sofa. Seve Ballesteros is demonstrating his golf swing to Eamon Andrews, who is more interested in reading out his life story from the famous red book.

Use all your senses. Hear the scraping noise of Christopher Dean skating around and around on a frozen puddle. And remember the number code. It is not a room, so the code is zero (number shape = football). Imagine a large football in the garden.

Now move inside the house to the bedroom, where another group of guests are entertaining themselves.

Bedroom: Code number 1 (telegraph pole)

Ossie Ardiles 1901	Elizabeth Goddard 1957
Organ Grinder 1907	Sean Connery 1963
Alastair Burnet 1912	Sherlock Holmes 1968
Adolf Hitler 1918	Gerard Depardieu 1974
Barry Norman 1929	Harry Enfield 1985
Clint Eastwood 1935	Neil Armstrong 1991
Dominic O'Brien 1940	Nigel Short 1996
Delia Smith 1946	

I always find it fascinating to imagine the conversations that would ensue at this sort of party. What, for example, do you suppose Clint Eastwood is saying to Adolf Hitler ('Go ahead punk, make my day!') Barry Norman is filming Gerard Depardieu's sword. Sherlock Holmes is fascinated by Neil Armstrong's spacesuit, examining it with a magnifying glass. Delia Smith is showing me how to cook. And Nigel Short is teaching Sean Connery a thing or two about chess, although Connery has a gun trained on him under the table.

You can have great fun imagining scenes, but remember to link each character to their particular room. Imagine Alastair Burnet looking out of your bedroom window and reading the news; the chess match is taking place on your dressing table; the cables from Barry Norman's cameras are wrapped around your standard lamp. Incorporate little details about the room; Harry Enfield is complaining about your wallpaper ('You didn't want to choose a colour like that'). And don't forget the room code is 1. Incorporate the number shape (a telegraph pole) into the scene.

Here are the remaining rooms, the corresponding years and codes. Once you have assigned everyone to his or her respective room, you have got the code number for any year from 1900 to 1999.

Spare Room: Code number 2 (swan)

1902, 1913, 1919, 1924, 1930, 1941, 1947, 1952, 1958, 1969, 1975, 1980, 1986, 1997

Stairway and Hall: Code number 3 (handcuffs)

1903, 1908, 1914, 1925, 1931, 1936, 1942, 1953, 1959, 1964, 1970, 1981, 1987, 1992, 1998

Lounge: Code number 4 (sailboat)

1909, 1915, 1920, 1926, 1937, 1943, 1948, 1954, 1965, 1971, 1976, 1982, 1993, 1999

Kitchen: Code number 5 (curtain hook)

1904, 1910, 1921, 1927, 1932, 1938, 1949, 1955, 1960, 1966, 1977, 1983, 1988, 1994

Downstairs Bathroom: Code number 6 (elephant's trunk)

1905, 1911, 1916, 1922, 1933, 1939, 1944, 1950, 1961, 1967, 1972, 1978, 1989, 1995

The month code

The second stage is to get a numerical code for the month. Here is a list of the numbers for each month:

January	1	July	0
February	4	August	3
March	4	September	6
April	0	October	1
May	2	November	4
June	5	December	6

They are not difficult to remember. I suggest you use the number-shape method as an aide-memoire. Exercise your imagination to create a relevant image. Listed below are a few suggestions:

January (1)
No need for any visual mnemonics here. January is the first month of the year, hence 1.

February (4)
February reminds me of feBREWERY. I can visualize an old Thames barge unloading kegs of beer at a smuggler's inn. Using the number-shape method, boat = 4.

March (4)
Going back a few years, I can visualize an army of soldiers, maybe even Vikings, MARCHing a boat down to the water's edge carrying it on their shoulders. Boat = 4.

April (0)
Have you ever been caught in an April shower where

hailstones are the size of footballs? Nor have I, but I can imagine footballs falling from the sky, denting the roof of my car and bouncing in the road. Football = 0.

May (2)
I remember this by thinking that 'may' suggests a twofold choice: someone may or may not do something. I also think of makes of matches: Bryant and May and Swan Vesta. Combining the two gives you Swan and May. Swan = 2.

June (5)
I think of a landlady I know called Jane and I imagine her drawing back the curtains in the morning at her pub. Curtain hook = 5.

July (0)
Carrying on the pub imagery, I can picture the landlady looking out of the window at her scruffy daughter, Julie, kicking a football around on the dusty track outside the pub. Football = 0.

August (3)
I have a strong image of three ageing oak trees on an exposed hill top, swaying dangerously in A GUST of wind. They are fixed together by an enormous set of handcuffs, to prevent them from toppling over. Handcuffs = 3.

September (6)
I think of an elephant who has such a long trunk that it drags along the ground. It has become SEPTic. Elephant = 6.

October (1)
I picture an OCTopus sitting on top of a central telegraph pole, one with plenty of lines leading off from it. Telegraph pole = 1.

November (4)
I refer back to the image of the Thames barge unloading kegs of beer. At the front end of it, looking on with dismay, is a young NOVice, praying for the sins of mankind (or does he just want a drink himself?) Boat = 4.

December (6)
I imagine Father Christmas, naturally associated with December, riding into town on the elephant with a septic trunk. Elephant's trunk = 6.

You now have your codes for the various months. It doesn't take long to memorize them, and don't feel obliged to use my examples. Whatever you do, though, you must remember each number and its month. It's no good just remembering the list of numbers.

The day code

This is the easiest code of them all and is entirely self-explanatory. All you have to remember is that the week starts on a Sunday, hence 1, and ends with a Saturday, which you must call zero.

Sunday	1	Thursday	5
Monday	2	Friday	6
Tuesday	3	Saturday	0
Wednesday	4		

You will have noticed that all the code numbers fall somewhere between 0 and 6. This is because we are working in base-7. We are, after all, trying to calculate days of the week.

To establish the day code, take the date of the month, the 17th for example, cast out as many 7s as you can and see what you are left with. In this case, take 14 away from 17, leaving 3, which is the day code. If the date is less than 7, 3 for example, then 3 is your day code.

Once you have learnt these three codes (years, months, days) you are ready to calculate any day of the week this century.

The calculation

To work out the day of the week, simply add together the three codes: year, month, day. Once again, if the grand total is more than 7 (9 for example), simply cast out as many 7s as you can, leaving 2: a Monday.

Example 1:
22 October 1906

1. Day code: 22 cast out three 7s, leaving 1   =   1
2. Month code: October = OCTopus on telegraph pole   =   1
3. Year code: 1906 = OS = Omar Sharif playing bridge in garden   =   0

                       TOTAL: =   2

The total tells us the day of the week: 2nd.
22 October 1906 was a Monday.

Example 2:
31 August 1912
1. Day code: 31, cast out four 7s, leaving 3   =   3
2. Month code: August = A GUST of wind,
   handcuffs on oak trees   =   3
3. Year code: 1912 = AB = Alastair Burnet
   reading news in bedroom   =   1
                                        TOTAL: =   7

Because the total is divisible by 7, we are left with 0.
31 August 1912 was a Saturday.

Example 3:
New Year's Eve, 1999
1. Day code: 31, cast out 7s, leaving 3   =   3
2. Month code: December = Father Christmas
   on an elephant   =   6
3. Year code: 1999 = NN = Nanette Newman
   in lounge   =   13
                                          TOTAL: =   13

Take 7 away from 13 and you are left with 6.
New Year's Eve in 1999 will be a Friday.

When you get more proficient at the mathematics, you should cast out any 7s as you go along. If I were doing the above example, I would have added 6 to 3, making 9, and cast out 7, making 2, before adding 4.

Leap years

If a leap year is involved, you will sometimes have to make a slight alteration to the calculation. Leap years are divisible by 4 (1980, 1984, 1988, 1992, etc). Let us suppose the date you are asked is in a leap year and falls between 1 January and 29 February. In this case (and no other), simply subtract 1 from your final total. If the date falls within a leap year, but is outside January or February, simply carry out the calculation as before.

Example 4:
14 February 1952
1. Day code: 14, cast out 7s, leaving 0   = 0
2. Month code: February = feBREWERY =
   boat unloading kegs of beer   = 4
3. Year code: 1952 = Eric Bristow playing
   darts in spare room   = 2
                                        TOTAL: = 6

Subtract 1 from 6, because it is a leap year (and the date falls between 1 January and 29 February) and you are left with 5.
    14 February 1952 was a Thursday.

(Please note that the year 1900 was not a leap year. The only century leap years are those divisible by 400. The year 2000 will be a leap year.)

Doesn't this all take a very long time?
People are often puzzled when I tell them how it is possible to work out the day of any date this century. They see me do it in an instant and are then dismayed when they discover how much work is involved. In fact, it doesn't take long at all to come up with an answer. The more you practise, the quicker you get, and you must have faith in the ability of your brain to recall information virtually instantly.

Two tips

There are, however, two techniques that I use to give the impression of instantaneous recall. First, ask the person to repeat the data slowly. Second, start calculating the moment they impart the information.

For instance, as soon as someone says 'The 30th . . .' I am immediately casting out the 7s (four of them) leaving me with 2 ' . . . of September'. Again, I instantly think of SEPTic trunk, 6, add it to the 2 I already have, which makes 8, cast out 7, leaving me with 1. I am now already ahead of the question, waiting for them to say the year.

'1966.' Ah yes, 66 is SS, Steven Spielberg, who is in the kitchen. Kitchen = curtain hooks = 5 and bingo! 5 + 1 = Friday.

Barely has the member of the audience finished speaking than I have already given them the day of the week they were born on. They walk away confused, dazzled, or just depressed, unable to comprehend how I did it. Now you know!

How to remember the calendar of other centuries

Once you have become fluent with the codes, there is nothing to stop you from memorizing other centuries. You just have to learn one more set of simple codes:

```
1753-1799  =  4
1800-1899  =  2
2000-2099  =  6
```

What day was it on 24 November 1777?

1. Day code: 24, cast out 7s, leaving 3   =   3
2. Month code: November = NOVice praying
    on boat   =   4
3. Year code: 77 = GG = Germaine Greer
    burning bras in kitchen   =   5
4. Century code   =   4

                                            TOTAL: =   16

Casting out 7s, you are left with 2.
24 November 1777 was a Monday.

CHAPTER 11

. . . .

How to remember 'lost' chapters of your life

TIME TRAVEL

This brief chapter is for those who are frustrated by their inability to recall scenes from their childhood. It's also for anyone who likes the idea of fitness training, but can't stand jogging.

I am dedicated to the concept of exercise. Every morning I enter my mental gym (usually an easy chair) to put my imagination through a punishing programme of exercise. One of my favourite routines involves something I call 'time travel'. If I am honest, this particular 'exercise' is anything but exhausting: I find it incredibly relaxing and therapeutic. In fact, it's more like a sauna than a work-out, and yet it helps to tone or build up brain 'muscles'. Needless to say, it also works wonders for memory.

MEMORY AS THERAPY

Time travelling is all about returning to a particular time and location from your past and trying to recall everything in as much detail as you can. I suspect that we have all experienced that moment when happy memories of a previously forgotten part of our lives come flooding back. It's an exciting feeling but it can also be intensely frustrating: we can remember only bits of the past, glimpses that rapidly fade into nothing.

Time travelling helps open up whole vistas of your past life. It throws wide the shutters, shedding light on lost scenes and allowing you to re-live lost sounds, smells, textures, tastes and emotions. The past is an integral part of our character; it defines who we are. And although some events in our lives are best forgotten, there are many that are unwittingly and undeservedly confined to oblivion.

It is common for people in the immediate aftermath of bereavement, for example, to clam up and not deal with the loss for many years. Later on in life, when they have finally come to terms with it, they want to remember every detail about the person who died – their face, the sound of their voice, their scent, the happy times spent together. But a poor memory lets them down. Time travel can't bring people back to life, but it can animate memories and preserve scenes for posterity far better than any photo album.

I am also about to use it with someone who has lost her memory through an accident. Bit by bit, we hope to re-create her past, sketching rough outlines before filling them in with colour.

THE TECHNIQUE

Start by returning to a location that conjures up a number of varied, incidental recollections: your old school, an old friend's house you used to visit, or a village you left long ago.

Choose a specific starting point: it might be a flag-pole in the playground, a chapel pew, a treehut, a friend's kitchen. Look around you. What little incidents do you remember? How old were you then? What friends did you have? What were the typical noises? Traffic, trains, children playing?

Try to recall individual sounds characteristic of particular objects: the slam of a front door, a squeaky window, a creaky floorboard, a waterpipe that always shuddered. See if you can recall voices, even their timbre. If you are using your old school as a location, try to remember catchphrases used by teachers and pupils. Isolate particular events that took place, no matter how trivial they seem now. They obviously meant something to you then.

Use all your senses. Can you recall the smell of a damp, musty room, or the aroma of your garden? And what about the smooth feel of a polished walnut table, or the rough texture of a pebbledash wall, the one you used to run your hands along on the way to school?

Association is at the heart of time travel. One memory sparks off another. After a while, an overall picture begins to emerge, not just of the physical layout but also of your state of mind. Were you happy? Optimistic? In love? Depressed? Naive?

The deeper you reflect, the more memories will be triggered off. Experiences completely forgotten will come flooding back. Eventually, if you work at it, you will be in the same situation as I am now: I never run out of memories.

Daily routine

Spend a little time every day reflecting on the same area of your past until you feel you have exhausted every avenue of retrieval. It's possible you never will.

Every time you return to the scene, you will be starting with a clearer, more comprehensive picture. It's a bit like assembling a jigsaw puzzle: each detail adds something to the overall image. Don't be surprised if you move the pieces around, making corrections in matters of detail.

I have just had to alter the layout in my parents' back garden. One morning I realized that a certain cherry tree I had recently 'rediscovered' had, in fact, been chopped down years ago. I suddenly recalled the sensation of tripping over its stump and stubbing my toe. In turn, that reminded me of our next-door neighbour – someone I had completely forgotten – and his tantrum when the tree crashed through his fence.

How far back can *you* go? I can recall shaking the wooden bars of my cot, aged two. My mother predicted that I would be a boxer one day, given the way I was developing my infantile biceps. She wasn't far wrong. I did get a pair of boxing gloves for my tenth birthday.

OTHER BENEFITS

Time travel borders on self-hypnosis, but it comes with no health warnings and you won't need the click of someone's fingers to wake you. When I relax in my sauna of early childhood memories, I adopt the same frame of mind I had all those years ago: carefree, innocent, untroubled. Only then do I realize how much my expectations and opinions have changed.

Time travel has many other benefits. One common symptom of people who don't know how to use their memories is the failure to recall dreams. It is nonsense to say that we don't dream. We all do, every night. It is the brain's way of filing away the thoughts it has had during the day. By exercising your memory regularly, you will begin to recall more and more dreams. (You might even have more wild and untamed dreams! No promises, though.)

Finally, you may wish to use the findings of your archaeological dig for one of your journeys. When I memorized thirty-five packs of cards, I needed thirty-five routes, many of them taken from my childhood.

CHAPTER 12

. . . .

How to learn languages

BACK TO SCHOOL

When I was at school, I just about managed to scrape through with passes in O level French and Spanish. I can't help feeling slightly resentful today about the way I was taught. The ability and good intention of my teachers is not in doubt, but I bitterly regret the methods they used.

If only I had learnt how to train my memory when I was thirteen rather than thirty! I am convinced that I would have sailed through all my exams with top grades, using the principles that you are about to discover. School life would have been so much more productive and enjoyable. The amount of study, for example, would have been halved, freeing up more time to devote to other subjects or interests.

Instead, I progressed with all the speed of a garden snail. I never looked forward to lessons, least of all to language classes. There was no incentive to study, no desire to remember. I felt overwhelmed by the sheer amount of information I was expected to learn, living in perpetual fear of 'vocab. tests' on a Monday morning.

And as for exams! At best they could be described as boring. Most of the time they were a nightmare.

My troubles were further compounded by the suspicion that I suffered from dyslexia. The written word was not my natural medium. I could never understand why people got excited about the prospect of lying on a beach with a good book. I equated books with work and effort; they represented the classroom. What chance did I have learning a foreign language if I couldn't even read my own?

RIGHT SIDE OF THE BRAIN

To cap it all, I was left-handed. Among other things, this meant that the right-hand side of my brain, which is more concerned with spatial co-ordination and creativity, dominated the left-hand side, which is more concerned with articulating speech and comprehending language. It might explain why my passion for music, art and sport far outweighed any desire I ever had to learn Spanish or German.

I am convinced that training my memory over the last five years has helped to develop the left-hand side of my brain, enabling me to become a good 'all-rounder'. My dyslexia has almost completely disappeared. I no longer have a fear of reading, and five years ago I could never have contemplated writing a book like this! Similarly, learning foreign languages has become so much easier.

VOCABULARY

During language classes at school, I was left with the

impression that we were expected to learn new words as best we could. There was no instruction or set procedure telling us *how* to go about fixing these strange new sounds in our head or converting them into English. I was told, for instance, that the Spanish for food was *alimento*. How was I to remember this word, and that it was masculine?

The teacher's job didn't extend to the nitty-gritty business of *learning how to learn*. No one taught me *how* to commit a large number of new and alien words to memory. The teacher was there solely to deliver the information and explain how the language worked. Without a vocabulary, however, grammar is useless. What good is it, as you stutter and stammer in a bakery, desperately trying to remember the German for 'bread', if all you can remember is how to decline the verb 'to bake'?

We tried to learn words parrot-fashion, monotonously calling them out in class, or staying up late, half-covering one side of a well-thumbed vocab. book. What a travesty, a terrible waste of time and money! And as far as I can gather, things haven't improved much today.

A NEW METHOD FOR LEARNING LANGUAGES

The method I am about to show you is so effective and simple that I would expect you to learn a new language in a matter of days and weeks rather than months and years. Foreign words can be learnt and memorized after just one reading at an accelerated rate of approximately 50 to 150 words per hour. This means that a basic vocabulary of 2,000 words could be learnt after just twenty hours' study.

My personal best, using this method, is 320 new German words in an hour (after one sighting of each word). In the 1991 MEMORIAD, I won the language event by memorizing the most number of Chinese words in fifteen minutes. Not bad for a dyslexic slow learner!

If ever a subject was tailor-made for my approach to memory then learning languages is it. When you learnt how to memorize a list, you used location in the form of a simple journey. You used location again to remember names and faces; if someone reminded you of John McEnroe, you imagined a tennis court. It won't come as a surprise, then, to discover that location is central to my method for learning languages.

THE METHOD

When you are memorizing a large vocabulary, you need somewhere to store everything, a place where words can be accessed quickly and easily. There's nothing worse than having a head crammed full of information. It's not that there is too much (your brain can store far more information than most of us will ever need), it just isn't ordered properly or organized well.

Step 1:

Choose a familiar town. The perfect way to store basic vocabulary is by using a detailed mental map of a town or village. Think of the sort of words you will be learning: shop, church, garage, door, car, road, house, room, chair. A town can encompass all these everyday words.

Step 2:
Use your imagination and association – two skills you practised in Chapter 2. Let the foreign word suggest a key image to you. For example, the German for a plate is *teller*. Your key image might be of a bank teller. Concentrate on the phonetic sound of a foreign word, rather than the way it is spelt. If some of your associations produce words that don't quite match the correct pronunciation, don't worry. You can add the finishing touches of accent and emphasis later.

Step 3:
Place your key image in an appropriate location, suggested by the English. You are likely to find a plate in a restaurant, so think of a particular establishment you know in your chosen town.

Step 4:
Combining your key image and location, imagine a bank teller counting out piles of money on a large plate in the corner of the restaurant.

Choosing your town

The advantage of using a mental map of your town as your filing system is that you can group various types of words together in different quarters or ghettos. Adjectives can all be put in the park, for example; action verbs (to run, to shout, to jump, to swim, and so on) can be found in and around the sports complex.

More importantly, however, it allows you to divide up words into their respective genders.

Welcome to the gender zone

In Spanish and French, a noun is either masculine or feminine. Consequently, if I were learning either of these languages, my town would be split into two quite distinct zones or districts. If I were learning German, it would be split up into three zones: masculine, feminine, and neuter. *Teller* is a masculine word, so the restaurant where the bank teller is counting money would have to be in the masculine district.

It is important to spend time familiarizing yourself with your map before you start to fill it with images. Make sure you know which part of town is masculine or which is feminine, and which is neuter. If you were thinking of London, for example, everywhere south of the Thames might be masculine, and north of the river might be feminine.

Always use a separate town for each language, but this doesn't mean that two or three languages can't be learnt simultaneously. You are limited only by the number of towns you are familiar with. If it happens to be in the relevant country (Madrid, say, for Spanish, Paris for French, or Berlin for German), so much the better, but it's not too important.

Certain areas will build up with images more than others. You might find that there is a lot of vocabulary linked with a restaurant, for example. This isn't a problem; one image in the dining room might remind you of another. But make sure you are familiar with the many physical details of a popular location (the size, the layout, what is in the corner, etc), and don't let it get too congested.

Your town can expand if you need to include areas that don't exist on the real map. No planning permission is required. If there isn't a sports complex for all your action verbs, why not build one, or transfer one you know from somewhere else? And if your town doesn't have a park nearby, it should do!

Making a scene

Creating the overall scene that links the key image (suggested by the foreign word) with its location (suggested by the English meaning) is an essential part of the process. Generally speaking, the first association that comes to mind is the best one. Exactly the same principles apply as before: the more exaggerated and unusual the scene is, the more likely you are to remember it. Here are some examples of how I would remember German words:

Der Mantel (the overcoat):
Mantel makes me think of MANTELpiece, which is my key image. It's another masculine word, so I might as well stay in the restaurant (location). It is important to let your images spread organically through your town. Some might be next to each other; others might be across the high street, or round the corner. I imagine a huge, heavy overcoat hanging from the mantelpiece.

Using imagery in this way works well if you are

translating from English into German, or German into English. If I am searching for the German word for 'an overcoat', I immediately have an image of a huge, steaming one above a fire. It's resting on the MAN-TELpiece, which I know is in a restaurant in the masculine part of town, hence *Der Mantel*.

Similarly, if I am confronted with *Der Mantel*, I immediately think of a MANTELpiece (because my initial association was obvious) and an image of the steaming coat hanging off it.

Die Tür (the door):
My key image is of a sign saying 'detour' with a big arrow pointing left. It's a feminine word, so I go to somewhere in the feminine district of town where there is a door. The museum has a grand old oak entrance (location). I imagine that a big sign has been stuck on the outside of the door announcing a 'detour'. People are filing past, tut-tutting, as they make their way round to a side entrance.

I have to admit that this is quite a crafty one, because 'detour' sounds exactly like *Die Tür*. Even if you can't include the definite article in your image (and on most occasions you won't be able to), allocating words to specific districts makes remembering the gender very easy.

Schlafen (to sleep):
It's not easy to form an association with this word. My key image is of two city-types standing over a man who has fallen asleep. One of them is laughing loudly, the

other is saying, 'sssshhshhhh, you'll wake him'. 'Sssshhh' and 'laughing' approximately equate to *Schlafen*.

As *Schlafen* is a verb, I go over to the sports complex (location). The man has fallen asleep in a squash court.

With a little bit of imagination, you will always be able to find some link. It doesn't matter how far-fetched it is, providing that you will make the same connection in the future.

Die Gardine (the curtain):
My key image is of a beefeater 'guarding' something. As it's another feminine word, I go back to the museum (location), where there is a very valuable curtain hanging on one wall inside. I imagine the beefeater 'guarding' this old relic.

Das Glass (the glass):
In cases like this, where the German word is identical to the English, you should incorporate a code of some sort to indicate as much. I always use the image of a court jester or a joker (I am playing a wild card). It's a neuter word, so I make my way out of town to a suburb I have previously designated a neuter district. I know where there is a kitchenware shop (location), as likely place as any to find a glass. I imagine a court jester standing in the window, precariously balancing a Waterford cut-glass goblet on his head.

CONCLUSION

Pick a language and then establish the layout of your town, making sure to cordon off certain areas for different genders and word types. Let the words take you all around the town, spreading through your different districts.

See how quickly you can think of a key image for a foreign word, and then find a suitable location suggested by the English. Remember to combine them with an association. It's no good kidding yourself that you'll remember anyway. If you don't form a mental chain of links now, how can you expect to make the connection in a few days' time? It's like being given directions by someone in your car; if you are on your own later and you weren't concentrating the first time, you won't be able to find your way back.

I hope that this method removes some of the pain of acquiring a large vocabulary in a short space of time. You should find that it accelerates your rate of learning quite dramatically. If only I had discovered it when I was at school!

CHAPTER 13

. . . .

How to remember geographical facts

When I listen to the news on the radio, I am more likely to pay attention to an item on Ghana than on Liberia. Both share the same West African coastline, and both countries have English as their official language. The sole reason I express an interest in Ghana is because I have been there. It's an important difference.

A few years ago, I spent a short time in Accra, the capital. Located on the coast, it represents a tiny part of the country, but I now have several lasting key images of Ghana. Every time I hear or read about it, I immediately associate the news with one of them. For example, a story on the BBC's World Service about Bolgatanga in northern Ghana might remind me of the hotel I stayed at in Accra, 600 kilometres away. The image is quite irrelevant, of course, but it's enough to make me remember the story.

By contrast, I am not attentive to a news item on Liberia. There's no inherent reason why its affairs should be less interesting than those of Ghana. It's just that I've got nothing to go on. Until I have a key image of the country, Liberia will remain a word.

A DIET OF IMAGES

The ideal way to study geography would be to work your way around the world, building up accurate mental pictures of every country as you go. Sadly, this rather grand approach to learning is beyond most people's means, and we have been obliged to adopt less costly methods of studying the planet.

For example, the first thing we do when we want to find out about a remote country is look it up in an atlas. Even though it's two-dimensional, the image on the page helps the brain to process the information. The country is no longer just a word; it has shape and size. Not much, but it's a start.

We endeavour to get our bearings from other sources as well, building up a portfolio of images from newspapers, magazines, and TV. A glossy Sunday supplement full of gut-wrenching photographs of a drought in Sudan might provide us with our only image of the country. A TV drama on the battle for Goose Green might leave us with our only mental picture of the Falkland Islands.

Sometimes our sole insight into a country or city is through the eyes of a filmmaker. Our images of Italy might come from *Death in Venice*, or *The Italian Job*. A scene from *Out of Africa* could provide us with our one abiding picture of Kenya. Perhaps *The French Connection* is all we have ever seen of Marseilles.

Not surprisingly, we begin to forge crude associations between countries and their key national images. Mention Britain to a foreigner and they might well think of Big Ben. If I hear someone talking about Egypt, I immediately picture the pyramids. I am sure we all have key images for well-known countries: the United States, the Statue of Liberty; Australia, the Sydney Opera House; India, the Taj Mahal; France, the Eiffel Tower; Russia, Red Square; and so on.

However stereotyped and unfair these key images are, they serve a purpose. An association flashes across our mind every time the country in question is mentioned. The problems start when the mind is a blank, void of all images.

Visual deficiency of this sort makes learning geography particularly difficult. If we haven't visited a country, or read about it, or seen it on TV or in a film, how can we possibly be expected to remember facts about its capital, population, rivers, mountains, languages, religion, and culture? The brain craves mental imagery. Feed it!

A NEW METHOD FOR LEARNING GEOGRAPHY

Next time you are faced with learning large amounts of information about unknown places (the plight of most geography students), by all means turn to your atlas, but you should also turn to your imagination. As I said in Chapter 2, it is the key to a perfect memory.

Someone tells you, for example, that the state capital of Idaho in the United States is Boise. You have never been there in your life and you have no images of the place, from books, magazines, TV, or films. The chances are you won't retain the information for long.

If, however, you use your imagination to create your own key image, based on simple associations suggested

116

by the words themselves, the information is much more likely to stick.

To remember that Boise is the capital of Idaho, imagine an old lady called Ida (it's a very old-fashioned name) hoeing a flowerbed. A row of school boys are peering over her front wall, giggling behind her back.

Or take another example: you want to remember that the capital of South Dakota is Pierre. This time, a key image of the state flashes across your mind: the famous rock sculptures, known as the Mount Rushmore Monument. Perhaps you've seen it in a magazine or in a film. It's a vague recollection, but it's enough to form a backdrop for your own image, which you are about to create. Look at the word 'Pierre'. What does it suggest? Imagine a seaside pier jutting out from the rockface carvings.

MENTAL WAREHOUSES

On those occasions when key images spring to mind, you should always use them to set the scene, however distant or hazy they may be. If none are forthcoming, and you have to invent your own key image, you must be a little more resourceful in your choice of location. Try storing them all together in one place that has an unmistakenly American theme or feel to it.

The bar area from the TV series *Cheers* is currently a favourite 'mental warehouse' of mine. I have crammed it full of American facts that I can't deposit elsewhere. The old lady called Ida, for example, is now hoeing in the street, outside the bar window.

HOW TO REMEMBER THE STATES OF AMERICA
Have a look at the following list of American states and
their capitals. Displayed like this, they look a fairly
formidable prospect to learn. If you use your imagination, however, together with key images that you might
already have of the places, it becomes a relatively easy
task.

STATE	CAPITAL	STATE	CAPITAL
Alabama	Montgomery	Montana	Helena
Alasaka	Juneau	Nebraska	Lincoln
Arizona	Phoenix	Nevada	Carson City
Arkansas	Little Rock	New Hampshire	Concord
California	Sacramento	New Jersey	Trenton
Colorado	Denver	New Mexico	Santa Fe
Connecticut	Hartford	New York	Albany
Delaware	Dover	North Carolina	Raleigh
Florida	Tallahassee	North Dakota	Bismarck
Georgia	Atlanta	Ohio	Columbus
Hawaii	Honolulu	Oklahoma	Oklahoma City
Idaho	Boise	Oregon	Salem
Illinois	Springfield	Pennsylvania	Harrisburg
Indiana	Indianapolis	Rhode Island	Providence
Iowa	Des Moines	South Carolina	Columbia
Kansas	Topeka	South Dakota	Pierre
Kentucky	Frankfort	Tennessee	Nashville
Louisiana	Baton Rouge	Texas	Austin
Maine	Augusta	Utah	Salt Lake City
Maryland	Annapolis	Vermont	Montpelier
Massachusetts	Boston	Virginia	Richmond
Michigan	Lansing	Washington	Olympia
Minnesota	St Paul	West Virginia	Charleston
Mississippi	Jackson	Wisconsin	Madison
Missouri	Jefferson City	Wyoming	Cheyenne

Before you go any further, open a map of the United States. Console yourself by checking the whereabouts of the few states and capitals you already know. You've got a rough idea, perhaps, that New York is on the east coast and that Florida is further south. Stay with the coastline and take a wander. Try to orientate yourself by noticing where certain states are in relation to others. Do they border mountains, lakes, seas, other countries?

Make a note of any associations that spring to mind during this preliminary stroll. What key images are sparked off by the names on the map? New York, the Statue of Liberty perhaps; Arizona, the Grand Canyon; Kansas, the OK Corral; Nevada, the gambling halls; Florida, Disneyworld.

If you can't picture any, give your imagination a free rein. Let the words themselves suggest associations. It doesn't matter how bizarre your images are: the more unusual, the better. Is there any link between Helena and Montana? I happen to know someone called Helena. My key image is of her playing the card game Montana red dog (Helena/Montana). I can also imagine a fey-looking Santa Claus wearing a brand new Mexican sombrero (Santa Fe/New Mexico). My girlfriend Caroline is riding a Raleigh bicycle, heading north (Raleigh/North Carolina). And so on.

Once you have loosened up, it's time to concentrate on the list itself. Here is how I memorize some of the states and their capitals:

Jackson, *capital of Mississippi*

I have a good key image of the Mississippi river, so I imagine Michael Jackson trying to wade across it, struggling against the strong flow.

Frankfort, *capital of Kentucky*

No key images of Kentucky spring to mind. I do, however, immediately think of fried chicken and frankfurters. I therefore create my own key image of Colonel Saunders tucking into a hot dog. I imagine his perpetrating this traitorous act in a Kentucky Fried Chicken shop next door to the *Cheers* bar.

Albany, *capital of New York*

The Statue of Liberty is hard to beat as a key image of New York. I picture her with 'auburn' coloured hair. It doesn't matter if the association produces an imperfect match. 'Auburn' sounds sufficiently like 'Albany' to remind me of the name.

Tallahassee, *capital of Florida*

When I hear the name Florida, I always think of Disneyworld, which provides me with an excellent key image. I imagine a very 'tall' model of the dog Lassie, erected at the main entrance to the theme park. Again, the phonetic approximation of 'tall' and 'Lassie' is a sufficient reminder of the capital.

Austin, *capital of Texas*

I have a number of key images when I think of Texas: rocket launching, the Houston Astrodome, J. R.

Ewing's house, all of which make good locations. Austin makes me think of an Austin Maxi. I imagine a group of astronauts being taken to the space shuttle in a battered old Austin car, put-putting its way across the tarmac to the launch pad. (I also think of Austin Mitchell, the Labour MP. Perhaps he is wielding a Texas chainsaw in the *Cheers* bar . . .)

Juneau, capital of Alaska
TV news footage of the *Exxon Valdez* oil disaster left me with a number of lasting key images of Alaska's polluted coastline. Juneau reminds me of the actress June Whitfield. I imagine her helping to mop up some oil on the shore. Again, 'June' is a sufficient reminder of Juneau.

FADE TO GREY
Don't be worried about cramming your head full of bizarre images. Mnemonics of this sort are servants, and can be hired or fired at will. Their sole purpose is to act as aides-memoires until the information has been properly absorbed, at which point they will fade away, leaving the data firmly in place. Facts will soon be rolling off the tongue without a moment's thought: Boston, Massachusetts; Phoenix, Arizona; Columbus, Ohio. You certainly won't have to keep referring back to your galaxy of strange images.

USING A JOURNEY TO REMEMBER GROUPS OF COUNTRIES

South America
You are told to learn the capitals and population of all

thirteen countries in South America. Unfortunately, you have very little knowledge of any of them, so ready-made key images are thin on the ground. Time is also short, and this is how you are presented with the information:

COUNTRY	CAPITAL	COUNTRY	CAPITAL
Argentina	Buenos Aires	Guyana	Georgetown
Bolivia	La Paz	Paraguay	Asunción
Brazil	Brasilia	Peru	Lima
Chile	Santiago	Surinam	Paramaribo
Colombia	Bogotá	Uruguay	Montevideo
Ecuador	Quito	Venezuela	Caracas
French Guiana	Cayenne		

Faced with this sort of problem, you could do what you did with unfamiliar American states: form your own key images based on word association and place them all in a mental warehouse. One place, however, is likely to get a bit congested. A more efficient alternative is to store them using a simple journey.

Step 1:
Choose a familiar journey with thirteen stages, but this time try to make it a loop. In other words, you want to end up where you started, having travelled round a small circuit. The journey might be around a park or just around the block.

Step 2:
Have a look at your atlas. If you start with Venezuela at the top of South America, it is possible to work your way around all the countries going clockwise:

Venezuela, Guyana, Surinam, French Guiana, Brazil, Uruguay, Argentina, Chile, Bolivia, Peru, Ecuador, Colombia, and finally Paraguay, which is in the middle.

Step 3:
Look at each country and let the name suggest an artificial key image to you. Stay with the first association that comes to mind, however strange it may be, and don't worry if they are only rough approximations. This is what I imagine:

Venezuela	Venison
Guyana	Guy Fawkes
Surinam	Schoolmaster (Sir) with a nan bread on his head
French Guiana	Guy Fawkes wearing a beret
Brazil	Brazil nuts
Uruguay	Corned beef (Fray Bentos)
Argentina	Silver (argent)
Chile	Chilli peppers
Bolivia	Bowl of liver
Peru	Prune
Ecuador	*The Equalizer* (Edward Woodward/ TV series)
Colombia	Lieutenant Colombo (TV series)
Paraguay	Parachute

Step 4:
Once you have thought up your own key images, walk around your mental journey, placing them at each stage. Don't forget that Paraguay is the odd one out: it may come at the end of your journey, but it's really in the middle (having landed by parachute, of course).

Step 5:
Look at the capitals of each country. Think of the first image that comes into your head and combine it with your key image. For example, the capital of Venezuela is Caracas and my key image is venison. I imagine a deer with a cracker in its mouth at the first stage of my journey. Or Colombia; the capital is Bogotá and my key image is Colombo. I picture the lieutenant bogged down in tar at the twelfth stage of my journey.

Your own images will be far more useful than mine. Once you have finished, you merely have to review your journey every time you want to know the countries of South America, their capitals, and approximate location.

The European Community
Try doing exactly the same for the European Community. I expect that you know much more of the information than you did for South America, but it's a good way to plug any embarrassing gaps you may have in your knowledge.

COUNTRY	CAPITAL	COUNTRY	CAPITAL
Belgium	Brussels	Italy	Rome
Denmark	Copenhagen	Luxembourg	Luxembourg
France	Paris	Netherlands	Amsterdam
Germany	Berlin	Portugal	Lisbon
Greece	Athens	Spain	Madrid
Ireland	Dublin	United Kingdom	London

Choose a journey with twelve stages, starting with Ireland. Working clockwise around Europe, the order of the countries is as follows: Ireland, Britain,

Denmark, Germany, Italy, Greece, Spain, Portugal, France, Belgium, Netherlands and finally Luxembourg, the smallest and in the middle.

Even if you know all the countries, capitals, and their whereabouts, a journey helps you to remember exactly who is and isn't a member of the European Community. For those countries that do pose a problem, apply the same principles as before, using word association.

If you want to memorize information about other groups of countries, Africa for example, or the ever-burgeoning number of independent republics in the former Soviet Union, use more journeys. Alternatively, you can use an image of a department store. Assign each country a key image and then allocate them to a floor. Depending on the number of countries you want to remember, your department store could have a basement, ground floor, first, second, and third floors, each one covering two or three countries.

If possible, try to reflect the countries' geographical positions in the layout of your mental building: the further north they are, the higher their floor. It's not always easy, and you will sometimes have to settle for a rough approximation. Some countries might even end up being represented as stairways or fire exits!

HOW TO REMEMBER POPULATIONS

It's very easy to add further information to your images of countries and capitals. For example, if you want to remember that the population of Venezuela is 20 million, you just have to convert 20 into a person and incorporate them into your image.

Using the DOMINIC SYSTEM, 20 turns into Bill Oddie (2 = B; 0 = O). I imagine Bill Oddie pulling a cracker with a deer. Unless the populations are very small, always expect your number image to refer to millions.

To remember that the population of the United States is approximately 249 million, I split the number down in to 24 – 9. Using the DOMINIC SYSTEM, 24 becomes the weatherman Bernard Davey (2 = B; 4 = D). Using number shapes, 9 becomes a balloon. I imagine Bernard Davey standing rather sheepishly in the corner of the *Cheers* bar, holding a balloon. (Perhaps it's a weather balloon.)

THE WORLD'S LONGEST RIVERS

Have a go at learning the following twenty rivers. Memorize their length by converting the information into complex images. Using the DOMINIC SYSTEM, break the numbers down into pairs of digits, ascribing a character and an action to each.

RIVER	LENGTH (miles)	RIVER	LENGTH (miles)
Nile	4,160	Missouri	2,540
Amazon	4,000	Paraná	2,485
Chang Jiang	3,964	Mississippi	2,340
Ob-Irtysh	3,362	Murray-Darling	2,310
Huang He	2,903	Volga	2,194
Lena	2,734	Purus	2,100
Zaire	2,718	Madeira	2,013
Mackenzie	2,635	São Francisco	1,988
Mekong	2,600	Yukon	1,979
Niger	2,590	Rio Grande	1,900
Yenisey	2,543		

To remember that the Nile is 4,160 miles, I imagine David Attenborough (4 = D; 1 = A) running along the banks of the river. (Running is the action of Steve Ovett: 6 = S; 0 = O.)

If I want to remember more information, I just add the relevant images to my scene. To remind myself that the Nile is in Africa, I might introduce a bit of big game, a lion or two perhaps. (David Attenborough is used to them, after all.) And to remember that it flows out into the Mediterranean, he could have a deckchair and lilo tucked under one arm. He is rushing to the beach for a spot of sunbathing.

THE TEN LONGEST RIVERS IN THE UK

RIVER	LENGTH (miles)	RIVER	LENGTH (MILES)
Severn	220	Wye	135
Thames	215	Tay	117
Trent	185	Nene	100
Aire	161	Clyde	98.5
Ouse	143	Spey	98

Numerical data of any kind can always be broken down into constituent parts and then converted into memorable images. If I want to remember that the River Thames is 215 miles long, I imagine Bryan Adams (2 = B; 1 = A) at the Thames flood barrier, closing a huge iron curtain to stop the water from drowning London. (Using number shapes, 5 = curtain hook.)

Try learning the nine other rivers. There is no limit to the information you can memorize if you use a little imagination.

CHAPTER 14

. . . .

How to remember history

CONCEPTS OF TIME

What's going on in our minds when we think of historical dates? How do we know immediately, for example, that the year 1947 is later in time than 1923? I am certain that it's not just because we've learnt to count. Time is an abstract notion, and in order to perceive it, we try to give it some form of spatial representation.

How do you 'see' years? I have asked people this question many times. Initial replies range from 'I don't quite get your drift' to 'How can you possibly see a year?' After further questioning, most of my subjects admit to having some form of mental landscape, some way of perceiving years in chronological order. Here are a few of their descriptions:

Mr A: I suppose I see this century as a straight line running from left to right. On my far left is the year 1901. Directly in front of me is the year I was born. To my right is this year, and at the end of the line, to my far right, is the year 2000. The nineteenth century

128

runs in just the same way, only it is one line below. All previous centuries are progressively lower down the 'page'. The year 1AD is a dot on the ground to my left. A thick black line separates AD from BC. All BC dates are below ground level, deep underground.

Mrs B: I am standing on a wide step, which represents the current year. In front of me are more steps going forward, up to and ending with the year 2000. Behind me are steps of a similar gradient down to the year 1900. Below these there are steeper steps representing previous centuries. At the foot of them all is the year 1AD. Beyond that, there is a sheer drop.

Mr C: I see the present century in terms of a graph; it's like the side of a mountain. It begins down to the left of me with the year 1900, and peaks slightly to the right with the year 2000. Beyond this, it's a misty plateau. Although it's always rising left to right, the gradient varies at different decades. There is a significant change at my birth year; it levels out dramatically for a moment. There are other subtle twists and turns, giving it an almost three-dimensional effect. In the forties, I can see puffs of smoke, commotion. The sixties I see as bright colours. The eighties is silver and fast. If I look a long way to my left, to the west, I can see the gradient continuing down through the centuries to 1AD. That area is rather like the foothills of a mountain. What lies beyond BC is unclear.

Having read these answers, ask yourself the question again: how do you perceive time? Perhaps you have some sort of symbolic landscape for the months of the year. I have talked to people who see individual months as part of a rising mountain, starting in the lowlands of January and ascending to the summit of December. Others see months in terms of a clockface: January is 1 o'clock, July is 7 o'clock, and December is midnight.

And what about the week? I talked to one person who visualized each day in terms of its position in his weekly planner. Someone else saw Monday as the beginning of a conveyor belt. Each day it moved forward to the weekend, whereupon it whipped round underneath to deposit them back at Monday. My own week looks like a playground slide. At the top is a Sunday, always the first day of my week. I begin slipping down slowly through Monday and Tuesday, speeding up to Friday before coming to rest at Saturday. I then walk back round again and climb up the steps to Sunday.

I hope that you are now beginning to understand your own perceptions of time. Weeks, months, years, this century, past centuries – it would seem that our minds desperately need some sort of symbolic landscape, some spatial image, to help with the conversion of an abstract notion like that of time into something more intelligible and relevant.

A simple journey is a good method for learning historical dates because it satisfies this desire for shape and form; it gives substance and structure to the mental landscapes we have already partially created for the past.

HOW TO USE A JOURNEY TO REMEMBER DATES

You are presented with the following list of twenty battles and wars and told to remember the whole lot in chronological order.

Twenty battles and wars

1066	Battle of Hastings
1314	Battle of Bannockburn
1415	Battle of Agincourt
1455	Wars of the Roses begins (ends 1485)
1588	Spanish Armada defeated
1642	English Civil War begins (ends 1645)
1805	Battle of Trafalgar
1815	Battle of Waterloo
1853	Crimean War begins (ends 1856)
1899	Second Boer War begins (ends 1902)
1914	World War I begins (ends 1918)
1916	Battle of Somme
1939	World War II begins (ends 1945)
1940	Battle of Britain
1945	Atom bomb dropped on Hiroshima
1950	Korean War (ends 1953)
1956	Suez Crisis
1962	Cuban Crisis
1982	Falklands War
1991	Gulf War

Choose a journey with twenty stages. Personally, I

would base mine in Hastings, a town I know well and a particularly appropriate place to begin. My route would weave its way through the various narrow streets of the Old Town, using different shops, houses, inns, and churches as stages. I would pass the tall sheds used by the fishermen for hanging their nets, walk along the beach, stop at a restaurant, pop into the theatre and finish up on Hastings Pier.

Whenever you are choosing a journey to learn information, try to ensure that it has some physical relevance to what you are memorizing. Not everyone knows the layout of Hastings, but there are many ways in which to incorporate the theme of war. Begin at a gun shop in the high street, or a local castle.

Run through the list, thinking of a key image for each conflict, and then place them at each stage. As ever, the first associations are the most important. They could be phonetic approximations, or something more obvious. These are mine:

	EVENT	KEY IMAGE
1.	Battle of Hastings	Arrow
2.	Bannockburn	Burning barn
3.	Agincourt	Gin bottle
4.	Wars of the Roses	Rose
5.	Spanish Armada	Sinking galleon
6.	Civil War	Sieve
7.	Trafalgar	Nelson's Column
8.	Waterloo	Train station
9.	Crimean War	Prison cell
10.	Boer War	Wild boar
11.	World War I	Muddy trench
12.	Somme	Poppy

13.	World War II	Churchill
14.	Battle of Britain	Spitfire
15.	Hiroshima	Explosion
16.	Korean War	Apple core
17.	Suez Crisis	Sewers
18.	Cuban Crisis	Pigs
19.	Falklands War	Lamb
20.	Gulf War	Burning oil well

Now use the DOMINIC SYSTEM to transform the dates into characters and actions, which can then be combined with your key images at each stage. For example:

1588 Spanish Armada defeated

My key image is of a sinking galleon, which I imagine at my fifth stage. I have organized my journey so that the fifth stage is the beach at Hastings. Using the DOMINIC SYSTEM, I break 1588 into 15 – 88, which translates into Albert Einstein (1 = A; 5 = E) and the action of wrestling (8 = H; 8 = H; HH = the wrestler Hulk Hogan). I imagine a galleon tilting dangerously, just off shore. A wrestling ring has been erected on deck, and Albert Einstein is fighting with a sailor.

1642 – 1645 English Civil War

My key image is a sieve and the sixth stage of my journey is a restaurant. I imagine a fight breaking out and customers grappling with each other, armed only with sieves taken from the kitchen. (An outbreak of 'civil' unrest, perhaps.) To remember that the war started in 1642, I use the DOMINIC SYSTEM to convert 16 – 42 into the unlikely image of Arthur Scargill (1 = A; 6 = S) rouging his cheeks (4 = D; 2 = B; DB =

David Bowie, whose action is putting on make-up). Perhaps his strange new look caused the rumpus. Anyway, he is making himself look pretty in the middle of the fight.

The DOMINIC SYSTEM can be used to memorize additional information. In this case, I also want to remember that the Civil War ended in 1645. I imagine Duke Ellington (D = 4; E = 5) playing the piano in the corner, oblivious to the scenes going on all around him.

1991 Gulf War against Iraq

My key image of the Gulf War is of a burning oil well, and the final stage of my journey is Hastings Pier. I imagine oil has been discovered on the coast and the pier has been converted into a rig. Unfortunately, it has been set on fire.

As the Gulf War is so recent, the only further data I need to remember is 91. Using the DOMINIC SYSTEM, this converts into Neil Armstrong (9 = N; 1 = A). I imagine him trying to put out the flames. He is wearing his spacesuit to protect himself from the heat.

HOW TO REMEMBER OTHER DATES USING JOURNEYS

A simple journey can help you to memorize large amounts of varied information. Try learning the following table, which lists the names of the twenty-six British prime ministers this century, the date they came to office, and their political persuasion.

Use exactly the same principles as before. Choose a journey with twenty-six stages. (You can always expand it to keep abreast of any dramatic developments.) Make your route relevant in some way; perhaps it starts in Downing Street, or at a number 10 in your road.

Run through the names, forming key images. Let the words themselves suggest associations if nothing else springs to mind. And use the DOMINIC SYSTEM to remember the dates. In each case, you can discard the '19' and just concentrate on the last two digits.

There is one further piece of information to learn: the political party. The easiest way to do this is by incorporating another key image:

Conservative	Bowler hat
Labour	Red rose
Liberal	Big woolly jumper
Coalition	Sack of coal

You can also incorporate colours (blue, red, yellow, black). Again, your own images are better.

British prime ministers this century

CAME TO OFFICE	PRIME MINISTER	PARTY
1905	Sir Henry Campbell-Bannerman	Liberal
1908	Herbert Asquith	Liberal
1915	Herbert Asquith	Liberal
1916	David Lloyd George	Coalition
1922	Andrew Bonar Law	Conservative
1923	Stanley Baldwin	Conservative
1924	James Ramsay MacDonald	Labour
1924	Stanley Baldwin	Conservative

1929	James Ramsay MacDonald	Labour
1931	James Ramsay MacDonald	Coalition
1935	Stanley Baldwin	Coalition
1937	Neville Chamberlain	Coalition
1940	Winston Churchill	Coalition
1945	Winston Churchill	Conservative
1945	Clement Attlee	Labour
1951	Sir Winston Churchill	Conservative
1955	Sir Anthony Eden	Conservative
1957	Harold Macmillan	Conservative
1963	Sir Alec Douglas-Home	Conservative
1964	Harold Wilson	Labour
1970	Edward Heath	Conservative
1974	Harold Wilson	Labour
1976	James Callaghan	Labour
1979	Margaret Thatcher	Conservative
1990	John Major	Conservative

American presidents this century

Test yourself further with American presidents, creating separate key images to distinguish between Republicans and Democrats.

INAUGURATION	PRESIDENT	PARTY
1901	Theodore Roosevelt	Republican
1909	William Taft	Republican
1913	Woodrow Wilson	Democrat
1921	Warren Harding	Republican
1923	Calvin Coolidge	Republican
1929	Herbert Hoover	Republican
1933	Franklin Roosevelt	Democrat
1945	Harry S. Truman	Democrat
1953	Dwight Eisenhower	Republican
1961	John Kennedy	Democrat
1963	Lyndon Johnson	Democrat

1969	Richard Nixon	Republican
1974	Gerald Ford	Republican
1977	Jimmy Carter	Democrat
1981	Ronald Reagan	Republican
1989	George Bush	Republican
1993	Bill Clinton	Democrat

USING RANDOM LOCATIONS TO REMEMBER DATES

A journey is not always the best way to remember dates. Faced with a long sequence of events or people, you will be hard pressed to find a more efficient method. However, there are occasions when we want to memorize individual instances in time, one-offs. The best way to remember these is by using random locations, as opposed to the ordered sequence of a journey.

Have a look at the following list of twenty-one useful dates:

1086	Domesday Book
1215	Magna Carta
1348	Black Death
1381	The Peasants' Revolt
1431	Joan of Arc burnt at stake
1476	William Caxton begins printing in London
1536	Dissolution of monasteries
1605	Gunpowder Plot
1665	Great Plague
1666	Great Fire of London
1750	Industrial Revolution begins
1752	Gregorian Calendar is introduced
1851	The Great Exhibition
1918	Women over thirty win right to vote
1926	General Strike

1945   Founding of United Nations
1948   National Health Service established
1953   Hillary and Tenzing conquer Everest
1969   Death penalty for murder abolished
1969   First man on the moon
1974   Britain enters European Community

If you were asked to memorize all of them in order, you would use a journey. For now, imagine that you are given one or two of these to learn during the course of a lesson, or a guided tour. This is how to remember them:

Step 1:
Let the words suggest a key image. For the Domesday Book, it could be a large, dome-shaped book. The General Strike might suggest a large banner; William Caxton suggests a printing press. Imagine a mountain for Hillary and Tenzing's conquest. And so on.

Step 2:
Look at the dates and convert them into persons and actions, using the DOMINIC SYSTEM.

Step 3:
Combine your images and place them at a relevant location. The dome-shaped book is in your local library. The printing press might be outside Wapping, by the main gates.

This is how I remember some of the dates:

1431 Joan of Arc burnt at stake
My key image is of a bonfire. Using the DOMINIC
SYSTEM, 1431 translates into Arthur Daley (1 = A; 4 =
D) and the action of weight-lifting (3 = C; 1 = A; CA
= Charles Atlas). My location is Shamley Green,
where I used to go on Bonfire Night. I imagine Joan of
Arc being burnt, while Arthur Daley practises a spot of
weight-lifting, seemingly unconcerned.

1536 Dissolution of the monasteries
My key image is of a church ruin. The year 1536
translates into Albert Einstein (1 = A; 5 = E) striding
out along a catwalk (3 = C; 6 = S; CS = Claudia
Schieffer, the fashion model). I imagine this strange
scene taking place in a church ruin I know.

1948 National Health Service established
My key image is of an ambulance. The year 1948
translates into Andrew Neil (1 = A; 9 = N) turning
into a mermaid (4 = D; 8 = H; DH = Daryl Hannah).
I imagine him being wheeled out of an ambulance in
front of our local hospital. DH is also an extra reminder
for Department of Health.

COMBINING JOURNEYS WITH RANDOM
LOCATION

You can, of course, choose a random location to
remember a date and then decide to store more information using a journey. For example, to remember
that the battle of Waterloo took place in 1815, you
might imagine Adolf Hitler (1 = A; 8 = H) writing on a

blackboard (1 = A; 5 = E; AE = Albert Einstein) in the middle of Waterloo station (your location). Further facts about the battle could be placed along a journey out of Waterloo. Each station on the Exeter St David's line, for example, going out through Woking, Basingstoke, Andover, could be a separate stage.

BRINGING THE PAST TO LIFE

If you want to increase your ability to retain historical facts still further, you can use familiar locations as a substitute for real ones. People you know can become famous figures of the past. All it takes is a little imagination.

CHAPTER 15

Popular mnemonics

A mnemonic is something that assists memory. (Mnemosyne was the Greek goddess of memory, and mother of the nine muses.) The most common forms are acronyms and verses, although my journey system could also be described as a mnemonic. In this chapter, I list a selection of the most common (and printable) ones: medical, historical, musical, mathematical, and legal.

It should be said that mnemonics don't meet with universal approval as a teaching method; academics dismiss them as exercises in idle wordplay, ditties for parrots who want to remember rather than understand. As far as I am concerned, there is nothing wrong with anything if it helps you to remember.

Having said that, I do wonder about the effectiveness of one or two of the following, some of which I have included solely for their literary quirkiness.

EXTENDED ACRONYMS

In the same way that we remember the name of an organisation by forming an acronym (UNESCO for United Nations Educational, Scientific and Cultural Organization), we often create meaningless sentences to remember useful pieces of information. The first letter of each word reminds us of what we want to recall.

This is how some people remember numerical prefixes (kilo-, hecto-, deca-, metri-, deci-, centi-, and milli-): **Kippers Hardly Dare Move During Cold Months**. The Great Lakes (Superior, Michigan, Huron, Erie, Ontario): **Sergeant Major Hates Eating Onions**. And musical sharps (F, C, G, D, A, E, B): **Fat Cats Go Dotty After Eating Bananas**. Food is a good subject for a mnemonic as we all like eating. As I said at the beginning of this book, we are more likely to remember those things we enjoy. It comes as no surprise, then, to learn that sex also plays its part in popular mnemonics. Most people have heard this way to remember the colours of the rainbow (red, orange, yellow, green, blue, indigo, violet): **Richard Of York Goes Battling In Vain**. But did you know how to remember them in reverse? **Virgins In Bed Give You Odd Reactions**.

The following two strike me as particularly odd, but then, mnemonics are intensely private affairs. **Did Mary Ever Visit Brighton Beach?** There's no answer to this question. It reminded someone of the order of social rank in Britain (Duke, Marquis, Earl, Viscount, Baron, Baronet). Then there is this strange comment, should you want to remember the order of England's Royal families (Norman, Plantaganet, Lancaster, York, Tudor, Stuart, Hanover, Windsor): **No Plan Like Yours To Study History Wisely**.

Doctors and nurses

Medics are famous for making up mnemonics. The amount of technical information they have to learn, particularly concerning the human anatomy, has inevitably led to some highly ingenious mnemonics. Sadly, most of them are unprintable, and those that are clean tend to be obsessed with women.

This one is used for remembering the nerves in the superior orbital tissue (lacrimal, frontal, trochlear, lateral, nasociliary, internal, abducens): **Lazy French Tarts Lie Naked In Anticipation**.

Stockings play a puzzlingly major role in medical mnemonics. I can only assume that the following two examples were invented shortly after the war, when developments in nylon legwear were raising eyebrows: **Should George Personally Purchase Ladies' Smooth Stockings?** A question on the lips of any self-respecting student who wants to be reminded from where the portal vein derives its blood (spleen, gallbladder, pancreas, peritoneum, large, small intestines, stomach). The following, rather desperate plea is a reminder of the branches of the abdominal aorta (phrenics, coeliac artery, middle suprarenal, superior mesenteric, renal, testicular, inferior mesenteric, lumbar, middle sacral): **Please, Can Soft Soap Remove Tint In Ladies' Stockings?**

Music

Music teachers are responsible for a whole host of mnemonics, born out of despair, I suspect, as they try to bang home the basics of musical theory to unwilling pupils.

Here is a selection of the most common ones used to remember the notes on a musical stave. Spaces (bass clef) (A, C, E, G): **All Cows Eat Grass**. Lines (treble clef) (E, G, B, D, F): **Every Good Boy Deserves Favour**. Sharps (F, C, G, D, A, E, B): **Fighting Charlie Goes Down And Ends Battles**. Flats (B, E, A, D, G, C, F): **British European Airways Deny Gentlemen Carrying Frogs**.

Snooker

Here is a simple way to remember which way you must set the green, brown and yellow balls on a snooker table: **God Bless You**. And for those who can't remember in which order you are meant to pot them (yellow, green, brown, blue, pink, black): **You Go Brown Before Potting Black**.

Mathematics

Mathematicians, like music teachers, seem to relish devising mnemonics.

Bless My Dear Aunt Sally! Believe it or not, this tells you the order of operations for complex mathematical equations (brackets, multiply, divide, add, subtract). There is an alternative, thought up, I suspect, by oppressed pupils. **'Ban Masters!' Demand All School-children**.

There are a number of ways to remember the first few digits of pi (3.14159265358979). In the following examples, the number of letters in each word denotes the corresponding digit.

How I want a drink, alcoholic of course, after the heavy chapters involving quantum mechanics.

Now I know a super utterance to assist maths.

How I wish I could enumerate pi easily, since all these (censored) mnemonics prevent recalling any of pi's sequence more simply.

The same method is used for remembering the square root of 2 (1.414): **I Wish I knew (the root of 2).**

A maths teacher named Oliver Lough devised this mnemonic to help his pupils with trigonometry: **Sir Oliver's Horse Came Ambling Home To Oliver's Aunt.** Read as SOH CAH TOA, it gives you the following:

Sin = Opposite (over) Hypoteneuse
Cosine = Adjacent (over) Hypetoneuse
Tangent = Opposite (over) Adjacent.

And this pronouncement from a physician takes us, once again, back to sex: **Virgins Are Rare.** It's a reminder that Volts = Amps x Resistance.

Rhymes

Rhymes and poems provide us with some of the oldest mnemonics. Most people know the first few lines of the following rhyme, but perhaps not all of it:

Thirty days hath September
April, June and November
All the rest have thirty-one
Excepting February alone
Which has twenty-eight days clear

And twenty-nine in each leap year.

This short ditty was devised to lessen the risk of embarrassing developments at the pub:

**Beer on Whisky, very risky,
Whisky on beer, never fear!**

History teachers have come up with their fair share of rhymes to remember important dates:

**Columbus sailed the ocean blue
In fourteen hundred and ninety-two.**

**The Spanish Armada met its fate
In fifteen hundred and eighty-eight.**

The fate of Henry VIII's six wives (Catherine of Aragon, Anne Boleyn, Jane Seymour, Anne of Cleeves, Catherine Howard, Catherine Parr) is remembered by the following two lines:

**Divorced, beheaded, died,
Divorced, beheaded, survived.**

But I wish someone would think up a way of remembering the names of each wife, rather than just their grisly ends. One of the most famous mnemonic poems of all provides an ingenious way to remember the kings and queens of England since 1066:

Willie, Willie, Harry, Stee
Harry, Dick, John, Harry three
One, two, three Neds, Richard two
Harry four, five, six, then who?
Edward four, five, Dick the bad
Harry's twain and Ned the lad
Mary, Bessie, James the Vain
Charlie, Charlie, James again

William and Mary, Anna Gloria
Four Georges, William and Victoria
Edward the Seventh next, and then
George the Fifth in 1910
Edward the Eighth soon abdicated
And so a George was reinstated
After Lizzie two (who's still alive)
Comes Charlie Three and Willie Five.

Rhymes have also played their part at sea. This one is good for anyone worried about collisions:

If to your starboard Red appear
It is your duty to keep clear
Green to Green or Red to Red
In perfect safety go ahead.

And here is an easy way to remember port and starboard:

No red port left.

I will finish with a limerick used by lawyers to remember, in Latin, that the law doesn't take small things into consideration.

> There was a young man called Rex
> Who had a small organ of sex
> When charged with exposure
> He said with composure
> De minimus non curat Lex.

. . . .

CHAPTER 16

How to memorize a pack of playing cards

MY LOVE OF CARDS

Cards are where it all started for me. Ever since I was a child, I have been fascinated with games – patience, poker, pelmanism, bridge. When I was learning to count, I used to say 'eight, nine, ten, jack, queen, king'. And if I ever saw a card trick, I took great delight in solving it, whether it was a feat of mathematics or sleight of hand.

My love of cards took a dramatic change of direction in 1987. In fact, my whole life changed direction. You certainly wouldn't be reading this book now if I hadn't tuned in to see Creighton Carvello, a psychiatric nurse from Middlesbrough, pull a devastating memory feat on live TV. Carvello managed to recall a pack of 52 playing cards in exact order, having studied them for just 2 minutes and 59 seconds. It was a new world. I was flabbergasted. My mind immediately set to work, desperately trying to fathom how he had done it.

What I found most incredible was his evident ability to memorize the cards in sequence. He had the cards dealt out, one on top of the other, and looked at each card just once. I knew from this that he did not possess a photographic, or eidetic, memory. Baffled but intrigued, I retired to a quiet room, armed with a pack of cards, and pondered the seemingly imponderable. I was certain Carvello's secret lay in the sequence of cards. I had also heard something about using a story as an aide-memoire.

THE BREAKTHROUGH

As I sat in my room, my mind wandered back to a recent business trip. I had been obliged to stay in Khartoum for five weeks, doing nothing very much. Most of my time was spent at the Sudan Club, a place for British expats, and I could still visualize in detail the exact layout of the place.

Searching for a way to remember the pack in front of me, I started to imagine the court cards – jacks, queens, kings – sunning themselves in deckchairs around the club pool, chatting to one another. I could picture a jack holding a spade in his hands, a queen dripping in diamonds. Gradually, these images began to remind me of people I knew.

I could soon picture up to ten characters around the pool, but it was getting confusing. So they began to spread out around Khartoum, places I had visited, shops, street corners, hotels. This was when I first started to develop the journey method, the prototype of what you learnt in Chapter 2. Little did I know that I was invoking the spirit of Simonides, the Greek poet who is attributed with inventing the art of memory, back in the sixth century BC. (For more on the classical method, see Chapter 26.)

I quickly devised a route that went around the club and out into the streets of Khartoum. The court cards were easy, but others proved more difficult. I remember thinking at the time that it seemed an almost impossible (not to say thankless) task trying to remember all the symbols and link them together in under 2 minutes 59 seconds. But I have a stubborn streak, and I had set my sights on beating Carvello's record.

After a couple of days, I could memorize my first pack of cards in 26 minutes, with eleven errors. It was an important landmark, despite being way off the record. From then on, nothing else mattered; the next three months were an object lesson in accelerated learning. An evolution was taking place. All day, every day, late into the night, I dealt myself card after card, pack after pack. I noted down times to the nearest second, analysed errors, substituted symbols and altered journeys.

The 8 of diamonds proved particularly difficult to remember. Its symbol changed from a feeling of peace to a cloud, to white doves, to a hot-air balloon and finally to Richard Branson (who flies them). In the end, all the symbols became people. Cards had become animated, as numbers would soon after them.

After three months of intensive study, I felt I had a new brain; my memory was in a respectable state, much as the body feels after regular exercise. Not only could I memorize one pack in less than three minutes, six packs shuffled together had become a doddle.

Since then I have gained entries into the Guinness Book of Records for 6, 20, 25 and 35 decks (1,820); on every occasion they were all shuffled together and I looked at each card only once. My record for one pack of cards is currently 55.62 seconds.

In this chapter I will show you how easy it is to memorize a pack of cards. If you were diligent about learning the numbers in Chapter 4, and are now carrying around 100 people representing 00 to 99, you have already done over three quarters of the work. Your first pack will probably take you half an hour. With a little practice and dedication, you should be able to get your time down to 10 and then 5 minutes. If you are able to do it in less than 3 minutes, you should seriously consider entering a memory competition.

ANIMATING THE CARDS

You must first assign a person to every card between ace and 10 (court cards will come later). Cards are essentially numbers; the easiest way to bring them to life is to translate them into pairs of letters, a technique you have already learnt.

Use the DOMINIC SYSTEM to provide you with the first letter. Taking ace to be 1, you have the letter A; 2 becomes B, 3 becomes C, and so on.

The suit provides you with the second letter. All club cards, for example, are represented by a C. Diamonds are represented by a D, spades by an S, hearts by an H.

The 2 of hearts thus becomes BH, the 5 of clubs becomes EC. Referring back to our list of people in Chapter 4, you know that the 2 of hearts is Benny Hill,

(2 = B; hearts = H; BH = Benny Hill) and the 5 of clubs is Eric Clapton (5 = E; clubs = C; EC = Eric Clapton).

Here is a table to show you how to get the letters for cards from ace to 10:

CARD	CLUBS	DIAMONDS	SPADES	HEARTS
1 (ace)	AC	AD	AS	AH
2	BC	BD	BS	BH
3	CC	CD	CS	CH
4	DC	DD	DS	DH
5	EC	ED	ES	EH
6	SC	SD	SS	SH
7	GC	GD	GS	GH
8	HC	HD	HS	HH
9	NC	ND	NS	NH
0 (ten)	OC	OD	OS	OH

Copy this list and write down the corresponding person alongside each card. I am not asking you to think up any new people; you should already have all the characters suggested by the letters listed above.

It is important to remember that the letters are merely stepping stones to get you to your person. After a while, you will find yourself making the leap without using the letters. When I see the 6 of diamonds, I don't see the letters SD; I don't even perceive the card as the 6 of diamonds; I automatically have an image of Sharron Davies, the swimmer, wearing a rubber ring.

When a good pianist sight-reads a piece of music, there is no time to convert the notes into letters; he or she just knows which keys the fingers have to play.

Similarly, with typing, talking, reading, driving a car, it becomes automatic with practice.

You must always recall the person's unique action and prop (Sharron Davies is wearing a rubber ring). Charlie Chaplin is flexing a cane; Eddie 'The Eagle' is on a pair of skis; Eric Clapton is playing his guitar. I can't stress enough how important these associated actions are; they help to anchor the person to his or her surroundings (location).

COURT CARDS

There is no need to translate the court cards into letters, as they are already people. Once again, let them trigger off associations with people you know, or with public figures. I have listed below some suggestions to help you, but come up with your own as well.

Personally, I associate clubs with aggression, diamonds with wealth, spades with brunettes, and hearts with sex symbols.

CARD	PERSON	ACTION
Jack of clubs	Jack the Ripper	Ripping
Queen of clubs	Margaret Thatcher	Swinging handbag
King of clubs	Saddam Hussein	Burning oil wells
Jack of diamonds	Gerald Ratner	Wearing diamonds
Queen of diamonds	The Queen	Writing out cheques
King of diamonds	Jean Paul Getty	Driving Rolls-Royce
Jack of spades	John Travolta	Dancing
Queen of spades	Liz Taylor	Popping champagne
King of spades	Ronald Reagan	Standing on podium

Jack of hearts	Jason Donovan	Wearing coloured coat
Queen of hearts	Cindy Crawford	. . . That's my secret
King of hearts	Paul Newman	Playing pool

THE IMPORTANCE OF PRACTICE

Test yourself to see if you know all the people. There is no point going on to the next stage, the journey, unless you can name the person for each and every card. Deal yourself a pack; ideally, you should be able to call out the name quickly, but this takes a bit of practice. To begin with, try to spend not more than ten seconds per card. Some names will always come easily, others will prove more difficult. Make a note of the ones that aren't sticking and try changing the person. And remember, you *must* think of the relevant action for each person. It will save time later.

THE JOURNEY

The easiest way to teach you how to place these people along a journey is if I show you how I do it. I have listed below the 52 stages of a favourite route of mine around the town of Guildford in Surrey.

1. Bookshop
2. Cinema
3. Telephone kiosk
4. Newsagent
5. Bank manager's office
6. Bank cashier
7. Macdonalds
8. Building site
9. Steps to Brasserie
10. Reception
11. Stairs
12. Upstairs restaurant
13. Piano bar
14. Marquee bar
15. Stage
16. Backstage
17. Graveyard
18. Multi-storey car park
19. Careers Office
20. Chinese restaurant
21. Castle gate
22. Castle

23. Pub saloon bar
24. Public bar
25. Steps down
26. Bus stop
27. Traffic light
28. Car showroom
29. Footbridge
30. River boat
31. Car park
32. Theatre
33. Department store
34. Bus depot
35. Cobbled footpath
36. Fish and chip shop
37. Railway bridge
38. Top of train
39. Train driver
40. Compartment
41. First Class
42. Loo
43. Station platform
44. Waiting room
45. Ticket office
46. Sports centre reception
47. Cafeteria
48. Swimming pool
49. Badminton court
50. Showers
51. Sauna
52. Jacuzzi

When I originally mapped out this particular journey, I imagined a bird's-eye view of the town and sketched out a rough route from one end to the other. I then pictured myself walking along the route in a logical direction, and wrote down all the familiar places I frequented which I thought would provide suitable backdrops for my imaginary cast of characters.

I am constantly devising new routes for myself (I had to use 35, each similar to the above, when I memorized 35 packs of cards) and I am surprised at how easy it is to remember every stage. But then, the surroundings I choose are always familiar. Guildford, for example, is my home town.

When you come to map out your own route, you must do the same. Choose somewhere you know well. You might want to begin with the ten stages around your house, which you learnt in Chapter 2, and then branch off to work, or to someone's house, or out into the park.

Go around the route roughly to begin with, and then write down all the places that might be suitable. Once you have 52 stages, learn them by heart. You too will be surprised at how easy it is to remember them. If any are causing you trouble, change them. Perhaps they are too close together, or not distinctive enough.

Once you are happy with the route, you are in a position to memorize your first pack of cards.

MEMORIZING THE PACK

Before I start on a pack, regardless of whether I am going for a world record or just exercising my brain, I run through the journey in my head with three things in mind:

1. I count each stage to make sure there are 52 in total.

2. I imagine each stage to be empty. There must be no sounds, no people: Guildford, for example, becomes a ghost town. This will ensure that any previous characters or items you might have memorized are wiped out. You are erasing the video tape in anticipation of new information.

3. I view each stage from exactly the same vantage point in my mind's eye; it's as though I am looking through old snap shots. For example, I am always standing outside the bookshop peering in through the

157

window. I am always at the foot of the Brasserie stairs looking up, never at the top looking down. This is important for continuity.

The first card

I am now ready to deal the first card. Before I turn it over, I visualize the first stage of the journey, in this case the bookshop. A vague recollection of the premises is sufficient. I then turn the card. Let's assume it is the 5 of hearts, which we know is Edward Heath (5 = E; hearts = H; EH = Edward Heath).

It is not unusual to find him in a bookshop. His action is conducting so I quickly form an image of him facing a shelf of books pretending to conduct an orchestra with a baton in one hand. Location and person must interact for the image to be memorable. This whole process takes me, on average, one second.

Your brain is bound to feel a bit stiff to begin with, but you should aim to do each card in fifteen to twenty seconds. I have been working out every day for the last four years. Remember to use as many of your senses as you can. Take your time if it is all proving too difficult. Loosen up with some stretching exercises; flex your memory; touch the toes of your imagination with a few fantasies.

The second card

As I turn the second card, I am already looking at the cinema. It is the queen of spades. I imagine Elizabeth Taylor uncorking a bottle of champagne (her action) in the foyer. (No doubt she is attending the premiere of her latest film.) I am covered in spray and can feel the stickiness on my clothes. It is not just Liz Taylor that I will be remembering later. I always associate her with uncorking a bottle of champagne, which is just as important.

The third card

The third card is the 10 of hearts, which we know is Oliver Hardy. Imagine him trying to get into the tiny telephone kiosk with a large plank of wood on his shoulder. Oliver Hardy's action is fooling around with a plank. Again, the plank is as vital as Hardy.

The fourth card

The fourth card is Christopher Dean. I picture him skating (his action) head-first into the newsagent. The pavement outside the shop is icy and I hear the scouring sound as the metal skates pass over it. The skating is essential. It might just be that this is all I can recall when you come past the newsagents later on. But it will be sufficient, providing Christopher Dean is the only skater among my cast.

And so on. As you can see from my route, the last three stops anticipate a certain amount of exhaustion on my part. When I am going for a world record, I am charging about the place, so it only seems fair that I should collapse at the end in a bubbling jacuzzi.

The finale

The last card just happens to be the queen of hearts. I can think of worse fates for a man than splashing about in the bubbles with Cindy Crawford. It can all end very differently, of course; I once had Henry Cooper in there with me, throwing aftershave about the place.

THE IMPORTANCE OF TRUST

One of the secrets of remembering cards at speed is trust. You are bound to ask yourself how quickly you can move on to the next stage. But how do you know when a person has sunk in? No light flashes, no bell rings. To be honest, you are never going to know for certain when something is secure in your memory; you have just got to go on trust.

The relationship between people and location is like two velcro patches. There are hundreds of little idio-syncrasies in each person (and their associated actions or objects); similarly, the stage on your route is full of physical details. The two usually end up being linked in only a couple of ways, much like the velcro patches that require only one or two linked hooks to stay together.

THE REVIEW

This is the moment of truth and it's always a slightly anxious time for me. It shouldn't be, though. All the hard work has been done and it is time to relax and reflect. Creating images is much more tiring than recollecting them in tranquillity. Sit back and let the images wash over you; they can't be forced. All you are doing is playing back a video tape. (I should point out that the time taken *recalling* the cards is not recorded by the *Guinness Book of Records*. My world record, 55.62 seconds, is simply the time I took to store the information. It is a feat of memory, not of oral delivery.)

What's happening in the bookshop? I am looking in (from exactly the same vantage point outside) and I can see somebody waving a baton around at some books, as if they were conducting: Edward Heath, 5 of hearts.

I am now in front of the cinema. I see a flash of dark hair, a bottle of something: Liz Taylor, queen of spades. I sometimes find that the bottle of champagne is sufficient on its own.

The images are now beginning to fly thick and fast: a plank jammed in the kiosk: Oliver Hardy . . . 'another fine mess you've gotten me into', 10 of hearts. Someone skating into the newsagents, grating on the pavement: Christopher Dean, 3 of diamonds.

Even today, I am still surprised at the speed and fluency with which these images return. As soon as I recall one card, the next two are queuing up ahead, beckoning me. On a good day, I can't deal out the cards fast enough.

When you begin to get quicker at placing the cards (under ten minutes), you should find that you are no longer having to set each scene in such detail. The whole process of creating and recalling images is rather like rushing to catch a train. You run past a noisy market stall, a busker, road works, and a coffee shop. But it's after you have collapsed in the train and are getting your breath back, that you begin to remember the details: the shouts of 'lovely fresh strawberries', *Annie's Song* being played by a flautist, feeling the compressor drill vibrating under your feet, the smell of freshly ground Kenyan coffee beans.

Have confidence in your wonderful memory. Trust it. You will be impressed by its ability to recall the images along your journey. Make a note of the trouble-makers; it's either the person or the place that is at fault. If they begin to cause you trouble regularly, change them. And if it's only one card you can't recall, you can always find it out by a process of elimination.

CHAPTER 17

. . . .

How to win (always) at *Trivial Pursuit*

As part of my recent promotional work, I was asked to memorize two editions of *Trivial Pursuit* – the Annual Edition and Genus III. There were 7,500 questions in total, on Geography, Entertainment, History, Art and Literature, Science and Nature, Sport and Leisure. If you have read Section 2 (History and Geography), it won't come as a surprise to learn that I memorized the answers using instant association and location.

Not everyone, I admit, might be taken by the idea of memorizing thousands of *Trivial Pursuit* cards, but the exercise is a good way of practising the techniques you have already learnt. For players of the game, particularly those who are fed up with always being beaten at Christmas, it is a sure-fire way of never having to lose again.

The task is not as daunting as it sounds. It took me only one read through to commit the answers to memory. Setting aside an hour and a half each day, I learnt them at the leisurely pace of three per minute. After a month, I had memorized all 7,500.

Unlike a pack of cards, however, I needed to store all this trivia in my long term-memory. Apart from anything else, it is a handy trick to have up my sleeve for live TV interviews. So I embarked on a systematic programme of revision, which I will explain at the end of this chapter. Today, I only need to run through the questions once every three months. Some people, though, still don't believe it's a feat of memory.

THE TALKING BRIEFCASE

I once spent the day at Hamley's toy shop in Regent Street, London, answering *Trivial Pursuit* questions chosen by the general public. If I got one wrong, the questioner would win £50; if I got a second question wrong, they would win £100; and if, God forbid, I got three questions wrong, they would stand to win £5,000 in cash! Questions were picked entirely at random and throughout the day there were queues of people desperate to try their luck and catch me out.

At one point, I noticed a man who studied me closely for five minutes, before joining the queue. He was particularly interested in my black briefcase, resting against my chair. I suspected a scene. Sure enough, when he eventually chose a card, he turned around to everyone and announced, 'Right, I want that briefcase removed before I ask a question.' An assistant dutifully obliged and moved the case ten feet behind me.

'Further back, please,' the man demanded. Only when the offending object was completely out of view, or should I say out of earshot, for it had become apparent that the man credited my briefcase with unnatural powers of communication, did he proceed to ask me a question.

The question came out as a mumble. I think he was concentrating more on what my briefcase might be saying. I asked him to repeat it and he turned, victorious, to address the audience, 'You see! Have any of you noticed how often he has to have the question repeated?'

Everyone stared at their shoes, as only the English can do when a public row breaks out. I finally established what the question was: 'How old was Anna Kournikova in May 1992 when she was described as the finest tennis prospect of the century?'

'Ten,' I replied automatically. The man threw down his card in disgust, and walked off saying, 'It's a fiddle, it's a fiddle.'

It wasn't, of course. He failed to appreciate the brief chain of mental events that had provided me with the answer. Two key words, 'Anna' and 'tennis', were enough to trigger an image of a tennis court (location) I had once played on in Hertfordshire. It was owned by a friend of mine called 'Annie'. I could vaguely see a man playing the piano on the tram lines: it was Dudley Moore from the film *10*. This strange image provided me with my answer.

Needless to say, nobody won any prize-money that day, and the insurer's £5,000 was returned safely to the bank.

THE METHOD

As I promised, almost all the hard work in this book came in the early chapters. The method for memorizing *Trivial Pursuit* cards is very similar to the technique you used for putting names to faces.

1. Seize on a key word (or words) in the question and let it suggest to you a random location. It doesn't matter how absurd it is, provided that the association is instant. You are simply trying to ensure that the next time you hear that key word, the same location comes into your head.

2. Take a look at the answer. Grab hold of any associated image that flashes across your mind. Again, it is essential that you stick with the first image.

3. Using your imagination, link the location and image together.

Examples

In the following examples, I am giving you my personal associations for the purposes of demonstration. Yours might be a good deal more imaginative!

Q: What material is the Cricket World Cup trophy made from?

A: Glass.

The key word is 'cricket', and the obvious location is Lord's Cricket Ground. (If you can't picture a famous setting, use a local pitch.) 'Glass' suggests an image of an expensive cut-glass bowl. Linking the two together, I imagine the bowl balanced precariously on the stumps at Lord's (Taverners' end); I hear the glass shatter as it is smashed by an unplayable off-cutter.

Q: Which country's coast witnessed the battle of Trafalgar?

A: Spain.

The key word is 'Trafalgar' which suggests Trafalgar Square as a location. I often use an image of a matador for anything Spanish. I imagine him waving a red rag in front of one of the lions at the foot of Nelson's Column.

Q: What is the alternative name for a cavy?
A: A guinea pig.

The key word is 'cavy'. This sounds a bit like cave. Most of us have visited a cave at some time in our lives. I would use a cave I know in Ireland as the location. The ready-made image of a guinea pig needs to be strengthened in some way. I imagine a huge family of guinea pigs emerging from the mouth of the cave.

The images for some questions and answers require a little more invention, but they are still based on immediate associations. Here is another example:

Q: What knot are you said to cut if you overcome a major difficulty?
A: Gordian.

The key words are 'knot' and 'difficulty'. When I hear the word 'knot' I immediately think of a certain estuary in Ireland where, as a young boy, I first came across knots. It's a very strong location for me. I spent a long, depressing day fishing for brown trout, and most of my time was taken up untangling my line. For my image, I split 'Gordian' into two, Gordon and Ian, which happen to be the names of two friends of mine. I imagine Gordon and Ian at the river bank, helping me overcome my difficulties with the fishing tackle. What's the first thing to enter *your* mind when you hear the word 'knot'?

The method works providing you seize your first association when confronted with a key word. By all means explore the association (it's a fascinating area, as anyone who has played word association games will vouch), but don't over-analyse why the word reminds you of a particular place. Trust that your mental chain of events, no matter how far-fetched, will repeat itself when you come to read the question at a later date.

In all the above examples, I have streamlined my final image to give me the answer and nothing else. Take the question I was asked at Hamley's. I was simply trying to get to the number ten. The year 1992 was irrelevant, as was the surname, Kournikova, and the fact that she was described as the finest tennis prospect this century was of no consequence at all.

If you ever come across information that is of particular interest to you, and you want to remember every detail, simply add the relevant elements to your overall image.

REVISION

If you want to memorize *Trivial Pursuit*, the Annual Edition is a good place to start. It has 1,500 questions. As I said earlier, you should aim to memorize them at a rate of three a minute. You may find it takes you considerably longer to begin with, but the process will speed up. In order for the information to be stored on a long term-basis, you must revise regularly.

Find your own level of retention. You might need to look at the cards again within minutes, or after twenty-four hours. Personally, my first revision takes place after forty-eight hours, and then I can retain the information for months on end. So far, I've never been caught out on a single question.

THE JONATHAN ROSS SHOW

I have had to remember some daft things in my time. I was once asked by Jonathan Ross to memorize the first word on every page of Jilly Cooper's novel *Polo* for his TV show. The paperback version consists of no less than 766 pages. I set about this unusual task by planning eight journeys, each with fifty stages. I would need 383 stages in total if I placed two words on each one. To make the words more memorable, I gave them symbols, usually people: 'and' became 'Andrew', 'the' became 'Thea', 'you' became 'ewe'.

I received the book the day before the show was televised. By mid-afternoon, I had memorized all 766 words.

Just before the show, copies of the book were handed out to 150 members of the studio audience. Each person was given a set page number. If they were chosen, they could call out their number and personally verify that I had memorized the right word.

Jonathan Ross explained to the audience before I came on that certain words had been chosen in preference to others, to avoid repetition of dull ones such as 'to', 'and', 'of', 'a', 'it', etc. As usual, there were the inevitable sceptics. No sooner had I walked on to the stage than someone at the back started shouting: 'Fix! Fix!'

It wasn't a good start, but the heckling triggered off the following series of images: 'Jim'll fix it' Saville jogging down a leafy lane in Surrey complete with fat cigar and chunky gold chains. He was at the first position on the second stage of the seventh journey.

Within three seconds of hearing the word 'fix', I told the audience to turn to page 703. There was a frantic rustling of pages and, sure enough, the first word at the top of that page was 'fix'.

Thankfully, my sceptic shut up after that, and I could continue to demonstrate my memory skills in front of a trusting audience.

• •

CHAPTER 18

Memory and sport

LEARNING THE FA CUP

If you are one of those people who like to know who won in the 1949 FA Cup final (Wolverhampton Wanderers), or which horse won the Grand National in 1909 (Lutteur III), then this chapter is for you. Before I go on, however, I must declare a lack of interest: I am not a football fanatic. I just happen to know the results of every FA cup match since its inception back in 1872 (when the final was held at the Kennington Oval and the Wanderers beat the Royal Engineers 1–0). As Leslie Welch discovered in the 1950s, this sort of sporting knowledge goes down very well with the public, which is why I include it in my stage act.

It's also incredibly easy to memorize if you use a simple journey. Each year of the FA Cup is represented by a separate stage. The individual teams and scores are translated into persons and actions.

CHOOSING YOUR JOURNEY

One of the journeys I use for football begins in the goal-mouth of our local ground. Because I have to carry around so many routes in my head, each one storing a different sort of information, it helps if the beginning of the journey is somewhere appropriate. The journey I use to store golfing information, for example, starts at a familiar golf course; the one for horse racing results begins at nearby stables; another for motor racing starts at a local garage, and so on.

Here are the first ten stages of my FA Cup journey, with corresponding years:

STAGE	YEAR	STAGE	YEAR
Goal-mouth	1901	Car park	1906
Centre of pitch	1902	Driveway	1907
Stands	1903	Ground entrance	1908
Changing room	1904	Petrol station	1909
Clubhouse	1905	Roundabout	1910

Personally, I use three separate journeys to remember the FA Cup, but there is no reason why you shouldn't use one long, epic route. I find that breaking it down into three helps me access the information more quickly.

First journey: results from 1872 – 1900. This is a normal 50 stage route, except that I start at the 22nd stage. Second journey: results from 1901 – 1950. A normal route with 50 stages. Third journey: results from 1951 – 2000. Another 50 stage route, allowing me to update the information as we progress towards the millennium.

This approach allows me to locate instantly, for example, the result of the 1984 final between Everton and Watford: I simply go to the 34th stage of the third journey. (Everton won 2–0.)

FORMING YOUR IMAGES

There are four basic pieces of information to memorize when you are learning the FA Cup: the year, the winner, the runner up, and the score. The year is taken care of by the stage (1903 is at the third stage); the other three pieces of information can be translated into a single complex image, the sort you formed when learning how to memorize numbers in Chapter 4. The process is very simple:

Winner, Loser, Score = Person, Action, Person.

The choice of person and action for the winner and loser is entirely up to you, but you should follow the same principles as before. Use your imagination, and let the names of the teams suggest people to you. The first association is the most important.

It might be someone you know who is a fan of the team in question, or even a star player, a manager, a chief executive. Some people think of Gordon Strachan when they think of Leeds United, or Mark Hughes when they think of Manchester United. The obvious action for Arsenal is firing a cannon, the club's symbol.

If your knowledge of the game is limited, your associations might be more tangential. I imagine Robin Hood when I think of Nottingham Forest, and the action of firing an arrow. For Crystal Palace, I think of Richard O'Brien, the presenter of TV's *The Crystal Maze*.

To remember the score, use the DOMINIC SYSTEM to convert the figures into letters, which in turn translate

173

into people. If the result is 3–2, for example, your person is Cilla Black.

The easiest way to combine person, action, and person in one complex image is by inventing a short storyline. So if Crystal Palace were ever to beat Nottingham Forest 3 – 2, I would imagine the bald O'Brien loosing an arrow in Cilla Black's direction. To make the scene more palatable, I would place an apple on Cilla's head.

Here are the results from 1901 – 1910, broken down into their constituent parts:

YEAR (Stage)	WINNER (Person)	LOSER (Action)	SCORE (Person)
1901	Tottenham Hotspur	Sheffield United	3 – 1
1902	Sheffield United	Southampton	2 – 1
1903	Bury	Derby County	6 – 0
1904	Manchester City	Bolton Wanderers	1 – 0
1905	Aston Villa	Newcastle United	2 – 0
1906	Everton	Newcastle United	1 – 0
1907	Sheffield Wednesday	Everton	2 – 1
1908	Wolverhampton Wanderers	Newcastle United	3 – 1
1909	Manchester United	Bristol City	1 – 0
1910	Newcastle United	Barnsley	2 – 0

And this is how I remember some of them:

1901   Tottenham Hotspur vs Sheffield United 3 – 1
Year: 1901. The first stage of my second journey is the goal-mouth at my local club, which denotes 1901. Winner: Whenever I hear Tottenham Hotspur mentioned, I automatically think of Bob, my agent. He's a

dedicated Spurs supporter. Loser: If no obvious association springs to mind, I rely on phonetics. The first
syllable of Sheffield United is 'Sheff', which makes me
think of a chef, whose action is cooking. Score: Using
the DOMINIC SYSTEM, 3–1 translates into Charles Atlas
(3 = C; 1 = A). Complex image: I imagine Bob dressed
in full chef's apron and wearing a big white hat,
preparing an enormous meal for a starving Charles
Atlas who is sitting in the goal-mouth.

1907   Sheffield Wednesday vs Everton 2 – 1
Year: The seventh stage (1907) is the driveway leading
up to the ground. Winner: To avoid confusion with
Sheffield United, I concentrate on the word 'Wednesday'. This gives me a clear image of actress Wendy
Craig. Loser: Everton reminds me of Eve; her action is
tempting someone with an apple. Score: Bryan Adams
(2 = B; 1 = A). Complex image: I imagine Wendy
Craig walking slowly backwards down the driveway,
tempting Bryan Adams with the lure of a crisp green
apple. He is on his knees in beseechment, singing
'Everything I do I do for you'.

1910   Newcastle United vs Barnsley 2 – 0
Year: The tenth stage (1910) is the roundabout. Winner: Success at last for Newcastle United. I picture one
of their most famous citizens, Spender, aka Jimmy
Nail. Loser: Barnsley makes me think of barn dancing.
Score: Bill Oddie (2 = B; 0 = O). Complex image: I
don't suppose that Jimmy Nail would readily accept an
offer to barn dance with Bill Oddie, but I imagine them

both doing a merry jig around the roundabout.

HOW TO STORE EXTRA INFORMATION

Sometimes there is more to the match than the final score reveals. In 1901, Spurs' 3–1 victory over Sheffield United was a replay, following a 2–2 draw. To memorize this extra detail, I imagine Charles Atlas (who is waiting for his supper, courtesy of Bob, my agent) beating on the goalposts crying, 'Order!'

In 1910, Newcastle were finally victorious after being runners up for three out of the five previous years. The 1–0 victory was, in fact, a replay, following a 1–1 draw. This sort of information is very easy to include in your complex image. All you have to do is add on an extra action to the storyline.

In this case, I imagine Bill Oddie being chased around the roundabout by a swarm of bees. This is the action of Arthur Askey, who represents 1 – 1 (A = 1; A = 1).

There is no real limit to the amount of facts that you can store. Enthusiasts memorize the entire line-up of each team, including substitutes, the goalscorers, the minute in which they scored, and no doubt the names of the referee's two children. If the will is there, it's perfectly possible. You just have to expand the geographical layout of your journey.

If you think all these images are ridiculous, I assure you that they are considerably more memorable than an uninviting mass of characterless facts and figures. I, for one, could not possibly begin to absorb huge amounts of raw, untreated information about football unless I used the techniques I have described.

Once you have committed the information to memory, you must spend some time revising. Replay your 'video tape' until you know the journey and all its little stories by heart. Highlight key landmarks along the way; they act as invaluable reference points when you want to access information quickly. If you automatically know where the 5th, 13th, 19th, and 26th stages are, for example, it makes locating the intervening stages so much easier.

If football's not your favourite sport, this method works equally well with other sporting information. You can use a simple journey to store data on horse racing, cricket, snooker, boxing, rugby, even haggis hurling if the facts are available.

REFERENCE TABLES

I have printed out below every FA Cup result since 1872, broken down into Year (stage), Winner (person), Loser (action), Score (person) to make it easier to memorize.

FA CUP RESULTS: 1872 – 1900

Year	Winner	Loser	Score
1872	Wanderers	Royal Engineers	1 – 0
1873	Wanderers	Oxford University	2 – 0
1874	Oxford University	Royal Engineers	2 – 0
1875	Royal Engineers	Old Etonians	2 – 0 (1 – 1)
1876	Wanderers	Old Etonians	3 – 0 (0 – 0)
1877	Wanderers	Oxford University	2 – 0
1878	Wanderers	Royal Engineers	3 – 1

1879	Old Etonians	Clapham Rovers	1 – 0
1880	Clapham Rovers	Oxford University	1 – 0
1881	Old Carthusians	Old Etonians	3 – 0
1882	Old Etonians	Blackburn Rovers	1 – 0
1883	Blackburn Olympic	Old Etonians	2 – 1
1884	Blackburn Rovers	Queen's Park Glasgow	2 – 1
1885	Blackburn Rovers	Queen's Park Glasgow	2 – 0
1886	Blackburn Rovers	West Bromwich Albion	2 – 0 (0 – 0)
1887	Aston Villa	West Bromwich Albion	2 – 0
1888	West Bromwich Albion	Preston North End	2 – 1
1889	Preston North End	Wolverhampton Wanderers	3 – 0
1890	Blackburn Rovers	Sheffield Wednesday	6 – 1
1891	Blackburn Rovers	Notts County	3 – 1
1892	West Bromwich Albion	Aston Villa	3 – 0
1893	Wolverhampton Wanderers	Everton	1 – 0
1894	Notts County	Bolton	4 – 1
1895	Aston Villa	West Bromwich Albion	1 – 0
1896	Sheffield Wednesday	Wolverhampton	2 – 1
1897	Aston Villa	Everton	3 – 2
1898	Nottingham Forest	Derby County	3 – 1
1899	Sheffield United	Derby County	4 – 1
1900	Bury	Southampton	4 – 0
1901	Tottenham Hotspur	Sheffield United	3 – 1 (2 – 2)
1902	Sheffield United	Southampton	2 – 1 (1 – 1)
1903	Bury	Derby County	6 – 0
1904	Manchester City	Bolton Wanderers	1 – 0
1905	Aston Villa	Newcastle United	2 – 0
1906	Everton	Newcastle United	1 – 0
1907	Sheffield Wednesday	Everton	2 – 1
1908	Wolverhampton Wanderers	Newcastle United	3 – 1
1909	Manchester United	Bristol City	1 – 0
1910	Newcastle United	Barnsley	2 – 0 (1 – 1)
1911	Bradford City	Newcastle	1 – 0 (0 – 0)
1912	Barnsley	West Bromwich Albion	1 – 0 (0 – 0)
1913	Aston Villa	Sunderland	1 – 0
1914	Burnley	Liverpool	1 – 0

1915	Sheffield United	Chelsea	3 – 0
1920	Aston Villa	Huddersfield Town	1 – 0
1921	Tottenham Hotspur	Wolverhampton Wanderers	1 – 0
1922	Huddersfield Town	Preston North End	1 – 0
1923	Bolton Wanderers	West Ham United	3 – 0
1924	Newcastle United	Aston Villa	2 – 0
1925	Sheffield United	Cardiff City	1 – 0
1926	Bolton Wanderers	Manchester City	1 – 0
1927	Cardiff City	Arsenal	1 – 0
1928	Blackburn Rovers	Huddersfield Town	3 – 1
1929	Bolton Wanderers	Portsmouth	2 – 0
1930	Arsenal	Huddersfield Town	2 – 0
1931	West Bromwich Albion	Birmingham	2 – 1
1932	Newcastle United	Arsenal	2 – 1
1933	Everton	Manchester City	3 – 0
1934	Manchester City	Portsmouth	2 – 1
1935	Sheffield Wednesday	West Bromwich Albion	4 – 2
1936	Arsenal	Sheffield United	1 – 0
1937	Sunderland	Preston North End	3 – 1
1938	Preston North End	Huddersfield Town	1 – 0
1939	Portsmouth	Wolverhampton	4 – 1
1946	Derby County	Charlton Athletic	4 – 1
1947	Charlton Athletic	Burnley	1 – 0
1948	Manchester United	Blackpool	4 – 2
1949	Wolverhampton Wanderers	Leicester City	3 – 1
1950	Arsenal	Liverpool	2 – 0
1951	Newcastle United	Blackpool	2 – 0
1952	Newcastle United	Arsenal	1 – 0
1953	Blackpool	Bolton Wanderers	4 – 3
1954	West Bromwich Albion	Preston North End	3 – 2
1955	Newcastle United	Manchester City	3 – 1
1956	Manchester City	Birmingham City	3 – 1
1957	Aston Villa	Manchester United	2 – 1
1958	Bolton Wanderers	Manchester United	2 – 0
1959	Nottingham Forest	Luton Town	2 – 1
1960	Wolverhampton	Blackburn Rovers	3 – 0

179

1961	Tottenham Hotspur	Leicester City	2 – 0
1962	Tottenham Hotspur	Burnley	3 – 1
1963	Manchester United	Leicester City	3 – 1
1964	West Ham United	Preston North End	3 – 2
1965	Liverpool	Leeds United	2 – 1
1966	Everton	Sheffield Wednesday	3 – 2
1967	Tottenham Hotspur	Chelsea	2 – 1
1968	West Bromwich Albion	Everton	1 – 0
1969	Manchester City	Leicester City	1 – 0
1970	Chelsea	Leeds United	2 – 1 (2 – 2)
1971	Arsenal	Liverpool	2 – 1
1972	Leeds United	Arsenal	1 – 0
1973	Sunderland	Leeds United	1 – 0
1974	Liverpool	Newcastle United	3 – 0
1975	West Ham United	Fulham	2 – 0
1976	Southampton	Manchester United	1 – 0
1977	Manchester United	Liverpool	2 – 1
1978	Ipswich Town	Arsenal	1 – 0
1979	Arsenal	Manchester United	3 – 2
1980	West Ham United	Arsenal	1 – 0
1981	Tottenham Hotspur	Manchester City	3 – 2 (1 – 1)
1982	Tottenham Hotspur	Queens Park Rangers	1 – 0 (1 – 1)
1983	Manchester United	Brighton & Hove Albion	4 – 0 (2 – 2)
1984	Everton	Watford	2 – 0
1985	Manchester United	Everton	1 – 0
1986	Liverpool	Everton	3 – 1
1987	Coventry City	Tottenham Hotspur	3 – 2
1988	Wimbledon	Liverpool	1 – 0
1989	Liverpool	Everton	3 – 2
1990	Manchester United	Crystal Palace	1 – 0 (3 – 3)
1991	Tottenham Hotspur	Nottingham Forest	2 – 1
1992	Liverpool	Sunderland	2 – 0
1993	Arsenal	Sheffield Wednesday	2 – 1 (1 – 1)

CHAPTER 19

. . . .

How memory can improve your golf swing

The attraction and frustration of sport is that there is always room for improvement. There are no absolutes. Sprinters can run the 100 metres faster, batsmen can score more runs, tennis players can play more passing shots, darts players can score 180 more frequently, and a golf ball can always be struck more sweetly.

Regardless of the sport, there are two fundamental ways in which you can improve your game: technique and practice. Memory plays a key role in both. Golf, like chess, is a game of the mind, requiring high levels of concentration and mental composure. A good memory is invaluable for players of all standards. Beginners need to remember a whole range of things before each shot (stance, grip, angle of clubface). And a professional, faced with an awkward lie perhaps, or difficult playing conditions, should always be able to refer back to a relevant precedent, possibly from many years ago.

I am going to concentrate solely on how memory can improve one aspect of the game: your swing.

DECLARATIVE AND REFLEXIVE MEMORY

If you are being taught how to drive a car, you are constantly trying to convert what the instructor is saying into physical actions. You make a conscious effort to remember the order of 'mirror, signal, manoeuvre', for example. Mental recall of this sort is known as 'declarative memory'.

In time, you will begin to check in your mirror, flick on the indicator and pull out without consciously recalling your instructor's words. Your actions become automatic and there is no longer any conscious act of recall. Memory, however, still plays its part and is known as 'reflexive memory'.

Similarly, if you are being taught how to drive a golf ball down the centre of the fairway, you are desperately trying to convert what the instructor is saying into a respectable shot. In those early, frustrating weeks and months, your technique relies heavily on your declarative memory: what were the instructor's ten key points? How was the man standing in the golfing video at home? And what did it say about grip in that book you got for Christmas?

Wouldn't life become so much easier if your declarative memory were able to absorb and recall all these tips in an instant? It would then be solely a matter of practice before they transferred into your reflexive memory. And think how much better your game would be if you could learn every piece of advice accurately.

It's very common for errors to creep in, and a poor technique becomes second nature just as easily as a good one.

A simple journey can radically improve the efficiency of your declarative memory. It gives you the best possible start if you are learning to play golf or rebuilding an aspect of your game. Nothing demonstrates this better than the golf swing, the bane of so many golfers' lives. Instructors are always encouraging players to tick off a mental checklist of dos and don'ts before each swing – easier said than done in the heat of a game. Using a journey, however, you can memorize a whole series of detailed instructions, effortlessly running through them whenever you want.

THE GOLF SWING

The person we have to thank for the golf swing as we know it today is Harry Vardon, the British professional who dominated the game at the turn of the century. He won the British Open six times and the US Open once. Before Vardon, players used the 'classical swing', hitting the ball long and low, but not very accurately. Vardon's style was to hit the ball higher in the air, causing it to land at steeper angle and stop more quickly. It resulted in much greater accuracy and gave rise to the 'modern swing' and the Vardon grip.

Little did Vardon know what angst he would cause budding golfers, or how much work he was creating for golf coaches. People have been trying to master the modern swing ever since. Nick Faldo has spent most of his life in pursuit of the perfect action. After years of constant re-evaluation and analysis, he has come closer than anyone to achieving it. He has had to carry out a witch-hunt to get there, isolating negative aspects of his game that have crept into his reflexive memory, and using his declarative memory to learn new techniques. The rewards of such dedication are there for everyone to see. Faldo, like Kasparov, is an example to us all.

GOLF LESSONS

One of the hardest things about golf lessons is trying to remember every pearl of wisdom handed down by your coach. It's not just a question of remembering what you are doing wrong, you must also remember the bits you got right! No matter how you are taught, the easiest way to recall all your coach's dos and don'ts is to draw up a mental list.

The entire action of hitting a ball (from takeaway to impact) takes less than two seconds on average, but there is a crowded sequence of events that must come together in perfect harmony if you want to produce the desired corker of a shot.

I don't pretend to be a professional (if only), but here is a typical list of the areas that coaches suggest you should keep an eye on during your swing:

1. Grip
2. Clubface aim
3. Ball position
4. Stance
5. Posture
6. Backswing
7. Top of backswing
8. Downswing
9. Impact
10. Follow through

In Chapter 2, you learnt how to memorize a list of ten items of shopping using images and a simple journey around your house. Treat this checklist in exactly the same way, except that I suggest you choose a route around your clubhouse. Allocate a different point to each stage: the car park covers your grip, for example; the changing room covers your clubface and the driving range covers ball position; the video booth covers stance; and so on.

With a little imagination, you can store as much information as you want at each stage. Take the restaurant (fifth stage), for example, which covers posture. You might form an image of a waiter taking your order in a peculiar way: he is bending down from the waist slightly, with the knees flexed and back fairly straight (or whatever posture your coach recommends). An outspoken manageress shouts across at you, 'Keep your head still when you're having your order taken.' And so on.

Alternatively, you might prefer to stick with one simple association. For example, you could imagine that Fred Astaire is in the video booth (fourth stage); the camera is filming him tap dancing, focusing on his lightning-quick feet. This reminds you to check your stance.

Every time you play a swing shot, you just have to run through your familiar journey, reminding yourself of all the points as you go. It doesn't take a moment – far less time than it takes to describe.

Using a journey gives you a better overall view of the shape and structure of your swing. It also gives you a solid framework of mental instructions that you can easily call upon during practice, allowing you to tweak and adjust every little aspect of your swing. After all, you are trying to ensure that only the purest instructions make their way from the declarative memory into your reflexive memory.

Other aspects of your game can also be stored at various locations around the clubhouse. To remember what your coach said about playing a downhill lie, for example, you could imagine a scene on some stairs. Tips on drawing the bali could be broken down and visualized along the driveway. All advice on bunker shots could be stored in the cellar. Apply the principles you have already learnt: use instant associations to translate the information into memorable images. The more unusual they are, the better.

CHAPTER 20

• •

How memory can improve your chess game

When he was asked what single overriding quality was required to become World Chess Champion, Garry Kasparov replied 'a powerful memory'. In 1985, he defeated Anatoly Karpov to become the youngest-ever world champion. He was barely twenty-two years old. Since then, Kasparov has been universally hailed as the greatest chess player who has ever lived.

A powerful memory can help players of all standards to improve their game. Beginners can learn simple opening moves and gambits, and club players can build up a bigger data base of previous games. Kasparov uses his memory to recall situations and moves from thousands of encounters he has stored in his head.

The following section is designed primarily for the beginner, but I also hope that the professional player will be interested in the economy of my method for memorizing a series of moves. An entire game, such as Boris Spassky versus Bobby Fischer in 1972 for example, can be recorded using a simple journey, with each stage representing one move.

HEALTHY BODY, HEALTHY MIND

A powerful memory is not all you need to become a chess champion. Kasparov is utterly dedicated to his profession, and trains mentally and physically every day. A typical morning might begin with a long cycle ride, followed by several lengths in a pool, before settling down to some work at the chessboard. He believes that if he stays physically fit, the quality and duration of his mental concentration is enhanced. Top-level matches are arduous affairs, requiring long periods of acute mental alertness.

I fully endorse this theory of healthy body, healthy mind. It applies to all mind-sports, not just chess. When I am preparing for a competition or attempting a world record, for example, I give up alcohol and embark on a rigorous schedule of running and cycling five weeks before the event. The effect on my concentration and performance is considerable. My body feels relaxed and I can think clearly and deeply. Sadly, though, the strict regime can sometimes fall by the wayside if I am successful, as I like to celebrate with a drink!

CHESS AND THE MEMORIAD

One of the events at the first World Memory Championships (MEMORIAD) in October 1991 was to memorize as many moves as possible from a game of chess. Moves had to be remembered in sequence. We were

188

each given five minutes to study the game and no mistakes were permitted. The moves were listed on a piece of paper and had to be remembered in sequence.

I managed to recall the first 11 moves. In chess, one move includes the repositioning of a white piece and a black piece. In effect, I had memorized the first 23 individual moves (12 white, 11 black) without error. This was sufficient to win the event and helped me to win the overall championship.

After the MEMORIAD, questions were raised about the legitimacy of using chess as a memory test. Critics argued that those competitors who had a sound knowledge of chess had a distinct advantage over those who had no experience of the game. Accomplished players were familiar with the board, enabling them to visualize moves and remember them more easily.

I appreciated these objections, but I also knew that neither I nor Jonathan Hancock, who came second, had been thinking of anything to do with chess as we memorized move after move. We had both been lost in our own mnemonic worlds, utterly divorced from the board and its pieces. While I was travelling around a castle in Ireland, Jonathan might well have been engrossed in *Alice's Adventures in Wonderland*.

ALGEBRAIC NOTATION

No one knows for certain who invented the game of chess. Sir William Jones, writing in his eighteenth-century essay 'On The Indian Game of Chess', suggested that it evolved in Hindustan. Known as 'Chaturanga', it consisted of elephants, horses, chariots, and footsoldiers. Chaturanga reached the Arab lands in the sixth century AD (where it became known as Shatrang) and was taken up in the West a century later. One thing we can be sure of is that the Arabs, in the ninth century AD, devised the now universally accepted method of recording chess games.

'Algebraic notation', as it is known, divides the chessboard up into vertical ranks of numbers (1 – 8) and horizontal columns of letters (a – h), giving each of the 64 squares its own co-ordinates.

The Chessboard

8	a8	b8	c8	d8	e8	f8	g8	h8
7	a7	b7	c7	d7	e7	f7	g7	h7
6	a6	b6	c6	d6	e6	f6	g6	h6
5	a5	b5	c5	d5	e5	f5	g5	h5
4	a4	b4	c4	d4	e4	f4	g4	h4
3	a3	b3	c3	d3	e3	f3	g3	h3
2	a2	b2	c2	d2	e2	f2	g2	h2
1	a1	b1	c1	d1	e1	f1	g1	h1
	a	b	c	d	e	f	g	h

The white pieces are set up in ranks 1 and 2; the black pieces are set up in ranks 7 and 8. Each of the main pieces is also given a letter:

King = K, Queen = Q, Rook = R, Knight = N, Bishop = B

All moves are represented by the co-ordinates of the square of arrival. Thus, if a White Knight moves from its starting position, b1 to c3, the move is recorded as Nc3. Or if a Bishop moves from c1 to a3, it is recorded as Ba3. There is no letter to denote a Pawn. If a Pawn moves from e2 to e4, it is economically recorded as e4.

It just so happens that the DOMINIC SYSTEM is perfectly suited to algebraic notation. The co-ordinates, consisting of one letter (column) and one number (rank), are already half-way to becoming people. A simple conversion of the number co-ordinate into a second letter will translate every one of the 64 squares into individual, memorable characters.

Using the DOMINIC SYSTEM, square c3, for example, translates into CC (c = C; 3 = C), which in turn translates into Charlie Chaplin. Square h2 becomes Humphrey Bogart (h = H; 2 = B); d7 becomes David Gower (d = D; 7 = G); and so on.

There is only one small alteration to make. When you first learnt the DOMINIC SYSTEM, I suggested representing 6 as an S rather than an F. Similarly, the f column on a chessboard should be represented as an S. Thus, the square f3 translates into Sean Connery (f = S; 3 = C).

I have printed out below 64 characters and their respective positions on the chessboard. As ever, your own people are preferable to mine.

THE DOMINIC CHESSBOARD

	a	b	c	d	e	f	g	h
8	Adolf Hitler	Benny Hill	Charlton Heston	Daryl Hannah	Edward Heath	Sherlock Holmes	Gloria Hunniford	Hulk Hogan
7	Alec Guinness	Bob Geldof	Charles de Gaulle	David Gower	Elizabeth Goddard	Stéphane Grappelli	Germaine Greer	Hughie Green
6	Arthur Scargill	Bram Stoker	Claudia Schieffer	Delia Smith	Ebeneezer Scrooge	Steven Spielberg	Graeme Souness	Harry Secombe
5	Albert Einstein	Brian Epstein	Clint Eastwood	Duke Ellington	Eddie Edwards	Stefan Edberg	Gloria Estefan	Harry Enfield
4	Arthur Daley	Bernard Davey	Christopher Dean	Dickie Davies	Eliza Doolittle	Sharron Davies	Gerard Depardieu	Humphrey Davy
3	Andy Capp	Bill Clinton	Charlie Chaplin	David Copperfield	Eric Clapton	Sean Connery	Gerry Cottle	Henry Cooper
2	Alastair Burnet	Betty Boothroyd	Cilla Black	David Bowie	Eric Bristow	Seve Ballesteros	George Bush	Humphrey Bogart
1	Arthur Askey	Bryan Adams	Charles Atlas	David Attenborough	Eamon Andrews	Susan Anton	Gary Armstrong	Howard Aiken
	a	b	c	d	e	f	g	h

Once every square has been assigned a person, the task of memorizing chess moves already looks less daunting. As far as I am concerned, Seve Ballesteros or Claudia Schieffer are much easier to remember than f2 or c6. However, the pieces themselves must also be assigned characters.

IMAGES FOR PIECES

Given the nature of chess pieces (they are virtually people), I suggest that you arrive at each person by focussing on the piece itself, rather than the letter. Here are my own people: King (K) = Prince Charles, Queen (Q) = The Queen, Rook (R) = Roy Castle, Knight (N) = Terry Waite, Bishop (B) = Archbishop of Canterbury, Pawn = no character required.

MEMORIZING AN OPENING EXCHANGE

It won't come as a surprise to learn that if you want to memorize a series of moves, you should use a simple journey. Each move, represented by a person, is assigned to a different stage. For example, if White opens by moving a pawn to b4, you imagine the weatherman Bernard Davey (b = B; 4 = D; BD = Bernard Davey) pointing at a weather map at the first stage of your journey. It follows that if you want to remember the opening six moves (i.e. six white moves, six black moves), you need a journey with twelve stages. Try memorizing these typical opening shots:

1. e4, e5
2. Nf3, Nc6
3. Bc4, Bc5
4. 0 – 0, Nf6
5. Nc3, 0 – 0
6. d3, d6

This is how I memorize some of them:

e4: Using the DOMINIC SYSTEM, e4 comes alive in the shape of Eliza Doolittle (e = E; 4 = D; ED = Eliza Doolittle). I imagine the cockney flowerseller at the first stage of the journey.

e5: I imagine Eddie 'The Eagle' Edwards at the second stage (e = E; 5 = E; EE = Eddie Edwards).

Nf3: Using the DOMINIC SYSTEM, this becomes Ns3 (f = s), which translates into *two* people: Terry Waite (N = Terry Waite) and Sean Connery (s = S; 3 = C; SC = Sean Connery).

The easiest and most efficient way to remember more than one person is to combine them in a single complex image (see Chapter 4). In this case, Ns3 translates into Terry Waite (person) wielding a gun, 007 style (Connery's action), at the third stage.

Once you have created your own images, replay the 'video', reviewing each scene as you go. It doesn't matter that someone like Terry Waite appears in a succession of images. The location is always different, and so is the action. It is very common for one player to shadow another in the opening exchanges, both moving their knights or bishops. You just have to make sure that each image is firmly rooted in its own particular location.

With practice, you might start to remember one move (black and white) at each stage, but I suggest you stick with half a move per stage until the process becomes second nature.

MEMORIZING SET PLAY

If a piece is taken, Knight takes Bishop say, it is recorded as N x B. Whenever this occurs, I imagine a fierce duel between the respective characters or some form of struggle (rather than forming a complex image). In this case, I would imagine Terry Waite locked in combat with the Archbishop of Canterbury.

If a player castles, it is recorded as 0 – 0. Using the DOMINIC SYSTEM, this translates into Olive Oyl.

The DOMINIC SYSTEM comes into its own when you want to remember whole games. I have listed two games below, one of them strictly for the beginners, and one for the pros.

Fool's mate

This is the shortest possible way of ending a game in checkmate, hence its name. In algebraic notation, it is recorded as follows:

1. g4, e6
2. f4, Qh4 MATE

Imagine a journey with four stages. If you are going to make a fool of yourself, you might as well do it on stage in front of an audience, so my route is based on a local theatre:

1. Theatre stalls
2. Orchestra pit
3. Stage
4. Backstage

Using the DOMINIC SYSTEM, this is how I memorize it:

White moves Pawn to g4. I imagine Gerard Depardieu (g = G; 4 = D; GD = Gerard Depardieu) charging through the stalls, cutting and thrusting at the empty seats with his glistening rapier. Black responds by moving Pawn to e6. I picture Ebeneezer Scrooge (e = E; 6 = S) counting his money in the orchestra pit. White moves a second pawn to f4. I imagine Sharron Davies (f = s = S; 4 = D; SD = Sharron Davies) swimming in a paddling pool. Black moves Queen to h4. I picture Her Royal Highness Queen Elizabeth II (Q) backstage, where the fuses have blown. She is sitting at a table, holding a Davy lamp (h = H; 4 = D; HD = Humphrey Davy) and trying to write a cheque (checkmate). Is she buying the theatre or paying her tax bill?

KARPOV versus KASPAROV March 1985

1. e4 c5 2. Nf3 e6 3. d4 cd 4. Nxd4 Nc6 5. Nb5 d6 6. c4 Nf6 7. N1c3 a6 8. Na3 d5 9. cd ed 10. ed Nb4 11. Be2 Bc5 12. 0–0 0–0 13. Bf3 Bf5 14. Bg5 Re8 15. Qd2 b5 16. Rad1 Nd3 17. Nab1 h6 18. Bh4 b4 19. Na4 Bd6 20. Bg3 Rc8 21. b3 g5 22. Bxd6 Qxd6 23. g3 Nd7 24. Bg2 Qf6 25. a3 a5 26. ab ab 27. Qa2 Bg6 28. d6 g4 29. Qd2 Kg7 30. f3 Qxd6 31. fg Qd4+ 32. Kh1 Nf6 33. Rf4 Ne4 34. Qxd3 Nf2+ 35. Rxf2 Bxd3 36. Rfd2 Qe3 37. Rxd3 Rc1 38. Nb2 Qf2 39. Nd2 Rxd1+ 40. Nxd1 Re1 + 41. Resigns.

CHAPTER 21

. . . .

How to memorize thirty-five decks

I was once given the task of memorizing the order of six separate packs of cards on a live TV show in Switzerland. Just before going on air, I made the fatal mistake of asking how many people would be watching. 'Oh, about 40 million,' said the producer nonchalantly, unaware of the terror he was instilling in me. The programme was broadcast right across Europe.

I was given my cue and duly stepped out onto the set . . . and into the homes of 40 million Europeans. It really was quite a lot of people. I started to memorize the decks. Everything went like clockwork until the host asked me to name the 42nd card in each pack. I couldn't stop thinking about the size of the audience. I was allowed one error throughout the whole ordeal, providing I corrected it immediately. There was prize money to be won (£3,500), but I was more concerned about not fluffing.

I correctly named the 42nd card in the first three decks, but when it came to the fourth deck, I called out the '2 of diamonds'. The audience audibly winced and the host said 'incorrect'. I just couldn't understand what had happened. The image in my head was crystal clear. I was seeing the 2 of hearts (a friend of mine who is always in the bath), but I didn't realize I was actually saying the '2 of diamonds'. A classic case of brain not connecting with mouth.

After an agonizing pause as I frantically re-grouped my thoughts, I spotted what was going wrong and called out the correct answer, much to the relief of the audience. I collected my prize and felt that I had earned it. Stress is a major cause of memory loss, which is why I always give myself more time for memorizing when I am performing in front of the camera.

TRICKS YOU CAN NOW DO

I mention this particular occasion to give you an example of the sort of tricks you can do, once you have learnt how to memorize a pack of cards in order. With a little concentration, you should be able to recite the cards backwards as well as forwards. You simply move along your journey in reverse order.

More impressive, I think, is the ability to sing out any card you are asked for: the 12th, the 39th, the 25th, and so on. This feat is easily achieved, providing you have reinforced certain stages along your journey.

If you look back to my route through the streets of Guildford (in Chapter 16), for example, you will notice that the 11th stage is a staircase. Whenever I am mapping out a new route, I always make sure that the 11th stage involves stairs. The 21st stage is always a door or gate. And I know when I am half-way, because the 26th stage is invariably a 'stop' of some kind. I use other markers for the 31st, 36th, 41st and 46th stages.

I avoid reinforcing the obvious stages (10th, 20th, 30th, etc) because no one ever asks me these! I find that people always try to catch me out by calling out odd numbers. But when someone asks what the 46th card is, say, I can tell them in an instant. And if they choose the 44th card, I either work back from the 46th landmark, or count forward from the 41st.

HOW TO REMEMBER MORE THAN ONE PACK OF CARDS

This is not as daunting as it might sound. For each new pack, I plan a new journey. When I memorized 35 packs of cards, I had previously mapped out 35 different routes. I don't expect many people to attempt 35 packs. You have to be slightly unhinged to put yourself through that particular agony. (It took me thirteen hours.) But if you do want to move on to multiple packs, there are one or two tips and pitfalls to look out for.

When I was attempting the world record, it took the invigilators half an hour to shuffle 35 packs. (There were 1,820 cards, after all.) Mathematically, there was a high chance of some anomalies appearing in the card sequence. I predicted identical cards grouped together, and others that might not turn up for ages.

In the event, there were 44 doubles (a jack of spades followed by another jack of spades) and one treble (9 of clubs, 9 of clubs, 9 of clubs). Some memory experts have complained of confusion when memorizing more than one pack, and I suspect this is because they are not using the journey method.

It allows you to place each character at a unique location. Michael Jackson dancing at a bus stop is a quite separate image from Michael Jackson dancing in front of the traffic at the lights. Besides, I find that any doubles (and particularly triples) that do arise are memorable in their own right because they are unusual.

If you are attempting more than one pack, you need to remember the order of your various journeys. I do this by incorporating a number shape at the first stage in each route. For instance, if my second journey is around Royston, a swan will feature in the first image (Swan = 2). Handcuffs (3) will start off the third journey, the fourth will commence with a sail (4); and so on.

The number of packs you can remember is restricted only by the number of journeys you can devise. You will be surprised at just how much information your memory can store and recall.

CHAPTER 22

. . . .

Number crunching

With training, many of us could walk from Land's End to John O'Groats, trek across the Antarctic, or even climb Everest. Very few of us, however, get around to achieving these goals; we are quite happy to watch others, content in the knowledge that of course we could do it too; we just don't want to.

The same could be said about memorizing large numbers. Not many people have the inclination to commit to memory the first 40,000 decimal places of pi, the current world record. The very notion of absorbing so many digits is utterly incomprehensible. And yet, I believe we all have the potential to perform feats of this sort.

This chapter is for those who want to learn how to crunch large numbers. It's also for those who cannot conceive how or why it's done and want to find out. I hope it removes some of the mystique, giving you an insight into what is, in fact, a very ordered and deceptively simple process. By the end of it, you will know how to memorize the first 100 digits of pi, and how to set about tackling bigger numbers.

EASY AS PI

It was on 9 and 10 March 1987, at the Tsukuba

University Club House, when Hideaki Tomoyori recalled the first 40,000 places in 17 hours and 21 minutes (including breaks totalling 4 hours 15 minutes) to set a new world record. In Britain, Creighton Carvello recited the first 20,013 places on 27 June 1980. It took him 9 hours and 10 minutes at Saltscar Comprehensive School, Redcar, Cleveland, to set the British record.

In the near future, I plan to set a new world record by memorizing the first 50,000 decimal places of pi. Pi (symbol π) denotes the ratio of a circle's circumference to its diameter. It is a very strange, almost transcendental number; it cannot be expressed as an exact fraction and there are no continuously recurring digits (unlike 10 divided by 3, which equals 3.3333333 etc.). Consequently, it makes for the perfect test of someone's memory of numbers, providing them with an infinite run of fiendishly random digits.

Here are the first 100 decimal places:

3.14159265358979323846264338327950288419716939937510582097494459230781640628620899862803482534211170679

Written out like this, the number looks fairly horrific. By applying the DOMINIC SYSTEM, however, you can turn this mountain of a number into a molehill.

Stage 1:
Choose a journey with 25 stages. Even though you are faced with a 100-digit number, you are only going to memorize 25 complex images, each one placed at a different stage.

202

Choose somewhere familiar for your journey and keep it solely for memorizing long numbers. I start my route at a patisserie, as good a place as any when you are remembering pi(e)!

Stage 2:

Break the number down into pairs of digits and translate each pair into a person, people or an action. (For the sake of example, I have used the list of characters and actions in Chapter 4.) Every four digits will be represented by one complex image. For example, take the first four decimal places: 1415. Break this down into pairs of digits: 14 – 15.

To form your complex image, translate the first pair of digits into a person, the second into an action.

In this case, 14 becomes Arthur Daley (14 = AD), and 15 is the action of writing on a blackboard (15 = AE = Albert Einstein, whose action is writing on a blackboard). Your complex image, therefore, is the sight of Arthur Daley scrawling complicated formulae on a blackboard. The prospect of memorizing 100 digits already seems less daunting.

I have written out below 25 stages of the route I use for memorizing 100-digit numbers, together with the digits, their persons and actions.

STAGE		PERSON		ACTION	
1	Patisserie	Arthur Daley	14	Chalking blackboard	15
2	Road	Nigel Benn	92	Playing tennis	65
3	Fountain	Clint Eastwood	35	Taking the helm	89
4	Jewellers	Gamal Nasser	79	Blindfolded	32

5	Car Park	Charlton Heston	38	Cooking	46
6	Fence	Bram Stoker	26	Performing magic	43
7	Orchard	Charlton Heston	38	Blindfolded	32
8	Stream	Gamal Nasser	79	Chewing thistles	50
9	Old Gunpowder mill	Benny Hill	28	Holding up Davy lamp	84
10	Bridleway	Andrew Neil	19	Playing rugby	71
11	Bridge	Steve Nallon	69	Writing	39
12	Windmill	Nadia Comaneci	93	Singing	75
13	Fish farm	Aristotle Onassis	10	Conducting	58
14	Gateway	Bill Oddie	20	Selling fruit	97
15	Manor	David Niven	49	Combing hair	44
16	Stonewall	Emperor Nero	59	Waving American flag	23
17	Lake	Organ grinder	07	Computing	81
18	Boathouse	Sharron Davies	64	Bridge	06
19	Old oak tree	Benny Hill	28	Playing golf	62
20	Steep hill	Oliver Hardy	08	Washing up	99
21	Church door	Harry Secombe	86	Milk float	28
22	Font	Oliver Cromwell	03	Becoming a mermaid	48
23	Congregation seats	Brian Epstein	25	Ice skating	34
24	Bell tower	Bryan Adams	21	Drinking Guinness	17
25	Graveyard	Omar Sharif	06	Riding a camel	79

You are probably thinking that the number on its own was preferable to this mass of data. But information presented in a linear form like this always looks more daunting than it really is. And as I have said before, an instant mental image often takes several lines to describe.

Despite appearances, the 100 digits have been translated into a series of images that the brain can accept and therefore store more easily. You are now in a position to start memorizing.

Shooting the script

Memorizing long numbers is a bit like making a mini-epic. You are the director, and a whole cast of actors, musicians, comedians, singers, stuntmen, and props are waiting to act out their scenes at a series of specially chosen locations. Here is my script:

Opening scene: 1415

Location: Patisserie (1st stage)

Person: Arthur Daley (14 = AD)

Action: Writing on blackboard (15 = AE = Albert Einstein)

I am obviously directing a comedy. Arthur Daley, as we saw earlier (in rehearsal), is writing something on a blackboard. He is standing in the middle of the patisserie, trying to flog a special recipe to the manager by chalking up its secret formula. I can feel the scraping sound on the blackboard (it gets me right in the teeth) and smell the delicious aroma of freshly baked pies.

Scene two: 9265

Location: The road (2nd stage)

Person: Nigel Benn (92 = NB)

Action: Playing tennis (65 = SE = Stefan Edberg)

Nigel Benn is practising his famous 'punch' volley. For some reason, he has erected a tennis net in the middle of the road and is oblivious to the traffic queuing up behind him. I hear the sound of the horns and smell the fumes. Benn is holding the racket slightly awkwardly in his bright red boxing gloves. He hits ball after ball. Perhaps it is just the camera angle, but he looks vast, towering above the net. Hundreds of fluorescent yellow balls are rolling down the sides of the road.

Scene three: 3589

Location: The fountain (3rd stage)
Person: Clint Eastwood (35 = CE)
Action: Standing at the helm (89 = HN = Horatio Nelson)

The advantage of directing big-cast movies is that you get to meet all the stars. In this dramatic scene, Clint Eastwood is wearing his usual deadpan expression and chewing on a cheroot, despite being soaked to the bone. He is standing in the middle of the fountain, where an enormous wooden wheel has been erected. The special-effects department have let me down. Eastwood is pretending to be Lord Nelson, battling with the helm in a raging storm. I feel wet as the spray drenches me as well. The whole scene looks like something out of a B movie, not the mini-epic I had intended.

Remaining scenes

And so it goes on. I am sure that with your own actors and journey, you can devise a series of far more amusing, off-beat and memorable scenes. Continuing with my film, Nadia Comaneci is singing from a wind-mill, Emperor Nero is waving the Stars and Stripes, and Benny Hill is up an old oak tree practising his golf swing. He's probably got his 'tree' iron out. An old joke, I know, but they are often the ones we all remember.

Finale: 0679

Location: Graveyard (25th Stage)
Person: Omar Sharif (06 = OS)
Action: Riding a camel (79 = GN = Gamal Nasser)

The final scene is a typically atmospheric shot, full of meaning and Hollywood dry ice. Graveyards are always misty, and this one is no exception. I see Omar Sharif in the distance, riding a camel. He is picking his way slowly through the tombstones and is wearing heavy, ghost-white make-up. I feel uneasy and cold. The mist is swirling and a full moon is up. Roll end credits!

REVIEWING

Once you have completed shooting on location, it is time to put your feet up and play back the film. Judge the results for yourself; you may need to do a little editing in places. If some scenes are too vague or confused, you may even have to call up the relevant actors and ask for a re-shoot.

If you are confident that all the scenes are equally memorable and are satisfied with the quality of the acting, you may decide you want to keep your home movie. (It is, after all, the first 100 digits of pi, and people won't believe it when you say you can recite them.) In which case, don't record over the journey. See it as your master tape, kept solely for remembering pi. After a couple of matinees, you'll soon know the story back to front, literally.

It shouldn't come as a surprise to learn that it is just as easy to recall the first 100 digits of pi in reverse. Watch the film carefully as you walk back along your journey, re-winding the tape. Each scene should come back just as easily, providing you have chosen a well-known journey. You might have to concentrate a little harder as you break down the complex images, but with practice you should be able to do it effortlessly.

Individual places

Once you are familiar with the positions of each stage (the 11th stage is a bridge, for example), you can start locating the position of any digit with impressive speed.

What is the 16th decimal place to pi? The first thing you did when you memorized pi was to divide up the 100 digits into 25 complex images, and locate each one at a separate stage. It follows that if you want to know which stage contains the 16th decimal place, you must divide 16 by 4.

You now know that it is the fourth stage, the jewellers, which contains the 16th decimal place. Breaking the scene down into its constituent parts, you have Gamal Nasser, who represents 79 (Gamal Nasser = GN = 79) and the action of being blindfolded, which

208

represents 32 (Cilla Black = CB = 32).

The 16th decimal place to pi is 2.

What is the 50th decimal place to pi? Divide 50 by 4 to find out the relevant stage. It must be the 13th, which is the fish farm. (The 12th stage covers the 45th, 46th, 47th and 48th digits; the 13th stage covers the 49th, 50th, 51st, and 52nd digits.)

Break the scene down into its constituent parts: The person is Aristotle Onassis (AO = 10). The action is conducting (Edward Heath = EH = 58).

The 50th decimal place to pi is zero.

BIGGER NUMBERS

With practice, you may become more ambitious and want to attempt even longer numbers. There are two ways to do this. You can either increase the number of stages on your journey, or expand the existing stages to accommodate a bigger complex image. If you have two persons and two actions at each stage, for example, you immediately double your storage capacity to 200 digits. Complex images of this sort are not difficult to form. In Chapter 4, you created ten-digit complex images to remember telephone numbers. Wherever possible, try to devise a simple storyline to link the persons and actions.

THE PI CHALLENGE

When I begin to memorize the first 50,000 decimal places to pi, I intend to have 50 separate journeys, each with 50 stages. Every stage will incorporate 5 people and 5 actions, linked by a story. In other words I will be allocating 20 digits to each stage: 50 x 50 x 20 = 50,000.

I find this the optimum geographical design, facilitating the location of any digit. For example, to find the 33,429th decimal place, I would initially take an overhead view of the 33rd journey (around the County of Cornwall), before dividing 42 by 2, to give me the 21st stage. I would then break down the complex image, locating the 9th digit, which in this case happens to be 7. I can make this calculation in seconds, possibly faster than it would take someone to instruct a computer.

Unlikely as it may sound, I intend to memorize the number quickly and painlessly, absorbing 4,000 – 5,000 digits daily over a two-week period. I will then recall the number in front of invigilators, hopefully breaking the world record, and finally erase it; 50,000 digits of pi is not the sort of information I want to carry around in my head long term.

I expect Mr Tomoyori or someone else similarly minded will gradually edge up the record. I predict that the first 100,000 decimal places to pi will have been memorized by the end of this century. Perhaps you are the very person to do it? The only problem I can foresee is finding invigilators who are sufficiently patient and willing to sit through such an event!

CHAPTER 23

• •

Remembering binary numbers

HEADS I WIN, TAILS YOU LOSE

I once bet a friend of mine that I could memorize the result of any number of coin flips as fast as he could spin the coin. He accepted the bet, thinking that he was on to a winner. A separate referee recorded the results: if it was tails, he wrote down 1, if it was heads, he wrote down 0.

After ten minutes, the referee had painstakingly written down the results of 300 coin flips. My friend thought that 300 would be a more than adequate number to win the bet. He was wrong. I was not only able to repeat the entire, monotonous sequence, but I could also locate instantly the result of any individual spin he chose. I could tell him, for example, that the 219th spin was a head.

I have to admit that there aren't many practical applications for memorizing 300 flips of a coin, other than taking money off gullible friends. But the ability to remember binary numbers, which is how I knew whether the coin was heads or tails, opens up a whole range of possibilities.

BINARY

Binary is the language of computers. It is one of the simplest ways of representing information because only two symbols, 0 and 1, are employed. Anything of a two-state, or dyadic, nature can be translated into binary: on/off, true/false, open/closed, black/white, yes/no, and even heads/tails.

Long binary numbers, however, are fiendishly difficult to remember. On the face of it, they would appear to present even more of a challenge than their base-10 cousins. Unless, of course, there is a way of bringing all those noughts and ones to life . . .

I have developed a system for memorizing binary that is an offshoot of the DOMINIC SYSTEM, in that it translates boring digits (and let's face it, in binary they are particularly dull) into persons and actions. Only this system is even more efficient. It allows you to remember a 12-digit binary number using just one person and action, brought together in a single complex image.

The task of memorizing 300 flips of a coin is thus made very simple. All I had to do was remember 25 complex images in a leisurely ten minutes – far less of a struggle than trying to recall 300 individual bits of meaningless information.

THE DOMINIC SYSTEM II

The first stage of translating a string of noughts and ones into people and actions is to break them down into a series of smaller groups, each one consisting of three digits. For reasons that will become apparent, you must

212

then ascribe a single-digit, base-10 number to each group.

There are eight different ways in which a 3-digit binary number can be ordered. I have listed them below, together with their new number:

000	=	0		
001	=	1		
011	=	2		
111	=	3		

110	=	4
100	=	5
010	=	6
101	=	7

Commit this code to memory. Use mnemonics to help you remember the various permutations. For example, 010 might remind you of an elephant – two ears either side of a trunk. (A trunk, you will recall, is a possible number shape for 6); 101 looks like a dinner plate with a knife and fork either side. (I happen to eat at 7.00 pm most evenings.) And so on.

You can now represent any 3-digit binary number with a single-digit base-10 number. It follows that 6-digit binary numbers can be represented by a 2-digit base-10 number.

For example: 011 = 2 and 100 = 5. It follows that 011100 = 25.

A 2-digit, base-10 number such as 25 is a far more attractive prospect to remember than 011100. Using the DOMINIC SYSTEM, you can translate it at once into a person: 25 = BE = Brian Epstein (2 = B; 5 = E).

Take another example: 111 = 3. It follows that 111111 = 33. Using the DOMINIC SYSTEM, 33 translates into Charlie Chaplin (3 = C; 3 = C).

COMPLEX BINARY IMAGES

The efficiency of the system becomes even more apparent when you want to memorize a 12-digit binary number. Using the DOMINIC SYSTEM, an ordinary 4-digit, base-10 number translates into one complex image. To remember 2417, for example, you imagine weatherman Bernard Davey drinking a pint of Guinness (24 = BD = Bernard Davey; 17 = AG = Alec Guinness, whose action is drinking a pint of Guinness).

Exactly the same applies when you are dealing with binary numbers. If 011100 = 25, and 111111 = 33, it follows that 011100111111 = 2533. Consequently, if you want to remember 011100111111, you just have to memorize the complex image for 2533; Brian Epstein flexing a cane (25 = BE = Brian Epstein; 33 = CC = Charlie Chaplin, whose action is flexing a cane).

When you look closely at a photograph in a newspaper or a magazine, you see a whole mass of tiny dots. Under a magnifying glass, they appear meaningless; it's only when you stand back that they 'condense' into a picture that makes sense. A similar process is going on here: you are reducing a whole series of meaningless noughts and ones into a single complex image.

Take another example. How would you set about memorizing 011011100111? It looks a fairly horrendous task until you start to break it down:

Stage 1:
Split the number up into groups of three digits:

011   011   100   111

Stage 2:
Ascribe the relevant code number to each group:

2   2   5   3

Stage 3:
Using the DOMINIC SYSTEM, translate each number into a letter:

B   B   E   C

Stage 4:
Using the DOMINIC SYSTEM, translate the first pair of letters into a person, and the second into an action.

Betty Boothroyd - Playing guitar
(BB)   (EC = Eric Clapton)

Your complex image is of Betty Boothroyd jamming on a guitar, which, I think you'll agree, is far easier to remember than 011011100111!

Here is a list of the 64, 6-digit binary numbers which you are now able to translate into characters (or actions). With these basic building blocks, you can go forward and tackle any large binary number.

Binary		Code		Letters		Character
000000	=	00	=	OO	=	Olive Oyl
000001	=	01	=	OA	=	Ossie Ardiles
000011	=	02	=	OB	=	Otto Bismarck
000111	=	03	=	OC	=	Oliver Cromwell
000110	=	04	=	OD	=	Otto Dix
000100	=	05	=	OE	=	Old Etonian
000010	=	06	=	OS	=	Omar Sharif

000101	=	07	=	OG	=	Organ Grinder	
001000	=	10	=	AO	=	Aristotle Onassis	
001001	=	11	=	AA	=	Arthur Askey	
001011	=	12	=	AB	=	Alastair Burnet	
001111	=	13	=	AC	=	Andy Capp	
001110	=	14	=	AD	=	Arthur Daley	
001100	=	15	=	AE	=	Albert Einstein	
001010	=	16	=	AS	=	Arthur Scargill	
001101	=	17	=	AG	=	Alec Guinness	
011000	=	20	=	BO	=	Bill Oddie	
011001	=	21	=	BA	=	Bryan Adams	
011011	=	22	=	BB	=	Betty Boothroyd	
011111	=	23	=	BC	=	Bill Clinton	
011110	=	24	=	BD	=	Bernard Davey	
011100	=	25	=	BE	=	Brian Epstein	
011010	=	26	=	BS	=	Bram Stoker	
011101	=	27	=	BG	=	Bob Geldof	
111000	=	30	=	CO	=	Captain Oates	
111001	=	31	=	CA	=	Charles Atlas	
111011	=	32	=	CB	=	Cilla Black	
111111	=	33	=	CC	=	Charlie Chaplin	
111110	=	34	=	CD	=	Christopher Dean	
111100	=	35	=	CE	=	Clint Eastwood	
111010	=	36	=	CS	=	Claudia Schieffer	
111101	=	37	=	CG	=	Charles de Gaulle	
110000	=	40	=	DO	=	Dominic O'Brien	
110001	=	41	=	DA	=	David Attenborough	
110011	=	42	=	DB	=	David Bowie	
110111	=	43	=	DC	=	David Copperfield	
110110	=	44	=	DD	=	Dickie Davies	
110100	=	45	=	DE	=	Duke Ellington	
110010	=	46	=	DS	=	Delia Smith	

110101	=	47	=	DG	=	David Gower

100000	=	50	=	EO	=	Eeyore
100001	=	51	=	EA	=	Eamon Andrews
100011	=	52	=	EB	=	Eric Bristow
100111	=	53	=	EC	=	Eric Clapton
100110	=	54	=	ED	=	Eliza Doolittle
100100	=	55	=	EE	=	Eddie 'The Eagle' Edwards
100010	=	56	=	ES	=	Ebeneezer Scrooge
100101	=	57	=	EG	=	Elizabeth Goddard

010000	=	60	=	SO	=	Steve Ovett
010001	=	61	=	SA	=	Susan Anton
010011	=	62	=	SB	=	Seve Ballesteros
010111	=	63	=	SC	=	Sean Connery
010110	=	64	=	SD	=	Sharron Davies
010100	=	65	=	SE	=	Stefan Edberg
010010	=	66	=	SS	=	Steven Spielberg
010101	=	67	=	SG	=	Stéphane Grappelli

101000	=	70	=	GO	=	George Orwell
101001	=	71	=	GA	=	Gary Armstrong
101011	=	72	=	GB	=	George Bush
101111	=	73	=	GC	=	Gerry Cottle
101110	=	74	=	GD	=	Gerard Depardieu
101100	=	75	=	GE	=	Gloria Estefan
101010	=	76	=	GS	=	Graeme Souness
101101	=	77	=	GG	=	Germaine Greer

Once you have familiarized yourself with the above (the recurring patterns make it easier than it looks), try memorizing a 60-digit binary number. Daunting though it may sound, you only need to remember five complex images, each one representing 12 digits. Choose a simple journey with five stages, and place each image at the corresponding stage.

For example, this is how I would memorize:

011101100100101101010110110010010101
0000000111001110111111001

Journey (Stages)	12-Digit Section	Code No.	Letters	Person	Action (Complex Image)
First	011 101 100 100	2755	BGEE	Bob Geldof	Skiing
Second	101 101 010 110	7764	GGSD	Germaine Greer	Swimming
Third	110 010 010 101	4667	DSSG	Delia Smith	Playing violin
Fourth	000 000 011 100	0025	OOBE	Olive Oyl	Playing records
Fifth	111 011 111 001	3231	CBCA	Cilla Black	Weight-lifting

A prediction

If, in due course, a record is set for memorizing the greatest number of randomly generated binary digits, I predict that it will be in the region of 150,000. Using my system, three binary digits are being represented by one base-10 digit; if I manage to memorize 50,000 decimal places to pi, 150,000 binary digits should be feasible. Similarly, I can currently memorize a 100-digit base-10 number in approximately 100 seconds. I am therefore able to memorize a 300-digit binary number in the same time. The race is on . . .

CHAPTER 24

. . . .

How to win at blackjack

Soon after I had learnt how to memorize playing cards, it occurred to me that there must be a way of cashing in on my new found ability. Blackjack seemed like a natural target. It involved skill (unlike roulette or dice, which are based on pure chance), and I was already familiar with the game. I also felt there was a score to be settled: I had lost many more times than I had ever won!

I had always thought that beating the bank was a romantic but ill-conceived notion – the stuff of fiction and a sure-fire way of losing even more money. It might be possible in a Graham Greene novel, but never in real life. Memorizing thirty-five decks of cards put a different complexion on things.

Today, I am barred from casinos all over Britain and France. One or two will let me in for a drink, but if I get anywhere near the blackjack tables, I am back out on the street. They know that I have devised a winning strategy, and if I played for long enough, I could break the bank.

I don't want to encourage anyone to take up gambling – there are many other ways of making money –

but my approach to blackjack is a good example of what can be achieved with a trained memory.

THE GAME

The object of blackjack is for the player to be dealt cards that add up to 21, or as close as possible, without 'busting'. The opposing dealer must draw cards totalling a minimum of 17. Whoever is closest to 21 wins that particular hand. The skill, for the player, lies in deciding how many cards he or she should draw, relative to the degree of risk.

As is my nature (my stubborn streak again), I wanted to work out whether it was possible to gain an edge over the dealer. I proceeded to deal myself thousands of hands, analysing every possible permutation. After six months, I had studied 100,000 hands.

I never intended to deal so many cards, but once I had started, I was overcome with a relentless urge to continue playing and amassing results. The only way to test theories satisfactorily was to carry out thousands of individual trials.

KEEPING IT IN THE FAMILY

You may find the thought of devoting so much time to a card game abhorrent, or at least a trifle excessive. I often wondered at the time what was really keeping me going. I think I now know, and it is quite uncanny.

After I had carried out all these experiments, I came across a 1932 newspaper article about the game of bridge. In December of that year, the London *Evening Standard* published a series of five articles by Dr E.

Gordon Reeve on the 'Reeveu' system for auction and contract bridge, invented by Gordon himself. In the article he says the following:

> Three years of illness gave me the opportunity to work out the possibilities of scoring game. I dealt 5,000 hands, and each hand was played by all four players – North, South, East and West, in all the denominations respectively. Thus, the results of 100,000 combinations of hands were tabulated.

It was a strange feeling coming across such a precedent; it was also comforting to know that I wasn't the only person fanatical enough to be lured into the monotonous world of card permutations. But imagine the shiver that went down my spine when I discovered that this man, whom I had never met (he died in 1938), was in fact my grandfather.

CARD-COUNTING

One of the first discoveries I made during my experiments was realizing that I would usually win if low cards had been removed from the deck. Conversely, if high cards (10s, court cards, and aces) had been removed, the bank won the majority of hands.

By keeping a constant check or tally on which cards had been dealt, I was able to judge, at any stage during the game, whether or not the conditions were favourable. If they were good (lots of low cards removed), I would stake large bets; if they were poor (lots of high removed), I would place the minimum bet.

This strategy is known as 'card-counting'. Card-counters are rife throughout the casino world. They are the scourge of club managers, even though they are not doing anything illegal. Most of them are small-time gamblers who nibble away at clubs' profits. They never win large amounts, but they still annoy the management. If they are spotted (most tables these days are monitored by sophisticated closed-circuit TV), they are usually asked to leave, and politely told never to darken the doors again. (Casinos are private clubs, allowing the management to reserve the right of entry or to rescind membership.)

Known card-counters are also likely to feature in the *Griffin Book*, a three-volume tome compiled by a Las Vegas detective agency. It is circulated world-wide among casino managers, and lists a variety of undesirables, everyone from trouble-makers to card-counters. I have never seen a copy, but I gather it includes photographs, stills taken from the security cameras.

HIGH ROLLERS

Set apart from the hoi polloi of small-time card-counters are a handful of supreme professionals, or 'high-rollers'. They can make upwards of £500,000 tax-free, annually. Utterly dedicated to their work, these are the card-counting elite. They operate either on their own or in small groups, and are virtually impossible to identify. They are always on the move, flying from one country to the next, constantly changing their identities and adopting a variety of disguises. Most of them are American or Canadian. Two are based in England. One, known as 'The Professor', lives in the Midlands and has been known to dress as a woman. The other, alas, has been forced to hand in his chips.

STAYING ON THE RIGHT SIDE OF THE LAW (OF PROBABILITIES)

After dealing 100,000 hands, I felt I had got to know the heart and soul of blackjack. Every aspect of the game had been dissected and held up to the light. I had developed a basic card-counting strategy to the point where the bank's overall advantage was reduced to a half of one per cent. In other words, for every £100 that I bet during the game, I would be returned £99.50, providing my stake remained constant ('flat betting').

If, however, I substantially increased my bet when the cards were favourable, I could realize a profit of £1 to £2 for every £100 of turnover staked. This might not sound a lot, but it soon adds up. If your initial stake is £100, for example, you can turn over £10,000 in an evening. It was time to put theory into practice.

I began by joining as many clubs as I could, all over the country. Profits were modest to begin with, but there were other perks of the job. I embarked on a pleasant tour of the casinos along the south coast, enjoying what I call 'free evenings': my profit would cover the cost of travel, meals, and drink.

It wasn't long before I was targeting the Midlands and certain London clubs, returning home every morning with a reasonable profit. The strategy was working. More important, the casino managers appeared to be tolerating my presence. I began to earn a good living, about £500 to £600 per week, and I was learning to ride the ups and downs.

I remember getting off to a particularly bad start on my first visit to a club in the Midlands. Within half an hour, I was £500 down. I decided that a good dinner was in order. After dining on a sumptuous steak, washed down with a delightful wine, I was pleasantly surprised to find that my dinner bill had been 'taken care of' by the manager. He had spotted a punter with potential. Managers do this from time to time, to encourage you to gamble even more money.

I returned to my blackjack table, whereupon I not only recouped my losses but ended up showing a profit of £500. I tried to share my delight with the manager, celebrating my change of fortune and thanking him for the delicious dinner. The look on his face signalled the beginning of the end of a beautiful friendship. After two more similar visits, I was barred.

It is hard to describe the thrill of placing heavy bets in a casino, especially a glamorous one, knowing that you have a clear advantage over the bank. But there were downsides to my chosen career. It's exhausting having to look over your shoulder all the time, waiting for the manager's discreet words in your ear, 'Mr O'Brien, could you come with me please.' (It wasn't always that polite.)

After a while, I was no longer satisfied with my earnings. It was small reward for a dangerous, itinerant lifestyle. I yearned for more and more profit and was soon taking home £1,000 per day. It was then that I became a marked man.

Word travels fast in the casino world. Scores of letters began to drop through the letter box, terminating my membership of casinos nationwide. 'Dear Mr O'Brien,' read one from a club in Luton, 'it has been decided at an extraordinary meeting of the Election Committee that your membership be withdrawn with immediate effect. This means that you will no longer be allowed to visit the club either as a member or as a guest.'

Many people think it is unfair to bar a player who merely beats a casino at its own game, particularly when there is nothing more than mental skill involved. I was doing nothing illegal. But I can understand the casino's point of view: they are in the business of making money, so why should they tolerate someone who reduces their profit margins? Besides, if I am barred, it is my own fault for making myself conspicuous in the first place.

BACK TO THE DRAWING BOARD

I was convinced that I was being barred because of my betting strategy. Most of the time, I would stake the minimum permitted amount (usually £5). When I calculated a clear advantage, however, I would raise it to £25, £50, or £100. Increasing it by a factor of twenty inevitably attracted the attention of the casino inspectors, but it was the only way I could capitalize on the odds. Or so I thought.

Back at the drawing board, I read all the best books

on the game and managed to acquire a print-out from Las Vegas listing thousands of possible hands and what to do in each situation. Using a computer, I proved and disproved every existing theory I could lay my hands on. This time, however, I was able to deal millions of hands in a matter of hours, thanks to the computer.

I finally arrived at an optimum strategy for winning, which I plan to publish in its entirety in a separate book. It requires a trained memory, a cool nerve, and simple mental arithmetic.

I will, however, disclose a few details now, to give you an idea of how it works. It's one of life's little ironies that I am no longer able to use it myself, although I did test it out recently on a lucrative tour of France's casinos (where my face was unfamiliar), but more of that later.

THE MOMENT OF TRUTH

As I said earlier, the card-counter's skill is to predict which cards are left in the shoe. People do this in a variety of ways, some more subtle than others. My approach, a variation on existing methods, is to assign a very specific value to each card as it is dealt. A high card has a minus value, and a low card has a plus value. (They range from approximately -2 to +2.)

As the shoe progresses, I keep a running total of the overall value, which I divide by a figure (anything between 1 and 8) reflecting the number of cards still to be dealt. This gives me what is known as a 'true count'.

In blackjack, you are required to place your bet before the cards have been dealt. If, after the previous hand, the true count is greater than +0.75. I will increase my bet for the next hand: the laws of probability tell me that the concentration of high cards still in the shoe has increased. If the true count drops below +0.75, I know that there is a greater concentration of low cards still to be dealt. High cards, remember, give me an advantage. Low cards give the dealer an advantage.

Let me explain a little more about the number that I use to divide the overall value of the cards. In Britain, one shoe of cards consists of four decks. The dealer will place a blank card somewhere near the end of the shoe. This is known as the 'cut', and it is where the dealing stops. Card-counters prefer the cut to be as close to the natural end of the shoe as possible, for reasons that will become apparent.

At the beginning of the shoe, I divide the overall value by 8. Let's assume the game has just started and only five cards have been dealt. They are all low cards and the overall value is +6. It would be foolish to conclude from a mere five cards that a high card is likely to follow, which is why I divide the value by so much. The true count then becomes +0.75 (8 divided by 6) and I don't increase my bet.

As the number of cards left in the shoe decreases, I divide by 7, then by 6, then by 5, and so on. In other words, the true count is calculated in proportion to the amount of cards remaining. (In France, where casinos play with six decks, I initially divide the pack by 12.)

Unless the croupier is inexperienced, you are unlikely to find yourself dividing by 1. The cut usually comes first. For the sake of example, though, let's assume that it is a very good cut and there are only a few cards left in the shoe. A lot of low cards have been dealt, so many, in fact, that the overall value is +12.

I would divide this figure by 1, still leaving me with a true count of +12 (an advantageous situation to be in). This means that there is a high concentration of court cards left in the few remaining cards still to be dealt. I increase my bet accordingly.

Using a finely calibrated 'true count' allows me to adopt a more inconspicuous betting strategy. All I need now is a good disguise.

TRACKING

My strategy incorporates many other technical features, most of which will not mean much to the uninitiated. 'Ace tracking', 'count tracking', and 'sequence tracking', for example, can all be mastered with a trained memory.

Sometimes an inexperienced croupier won't shuffle a shoe thoroughly. Imagine the advantage you would suddenly have if you had memorized sequences of cards from the previous shoe (a technique you learnt in Chapter 16 when you memorized one deck of cards).

UNORTHODOX CALLS

There are times when knowledge of the true count can lead to some very unusual calls. For example, let's suppose that my first two cards add up to 12, 13, 14, 15, or 16. The dealer's card, which is always face up, is a 2, 3, 4, 5, or 6. I know that the true count is -6; in other words, there are a lot of low cards left in the shoe. It's not a good situation for me, and the dealer is likely to win. Most players would stick.

Knowing that I am likely to be dealt a low card, however, I break with tradition and ask for more cards. Supposing the dealer has a 6 and I am on 13. I ask for another card, 5 say, and then stick on 18. The dealer takes a card, 6, and another, 5, making 17. I have won. If I had stayed on 13, however, the dealer would have drawn a 5, then a 6, making 17. I would have lost.

It doesn't always work like this, of course, but it's a way of making the best of a bad situation. Whenever I make strange calls, it always amuses me to hear the accusatory comments and criticisms from other players at the table. 'You're obviously new to this game, aren't you?' or 'Take my advice, if you want to win, never make a call like that.' Some people get quite upset and start claiming that my unorthodox calls are the cause of their ill-fortune.

STRATEGY NOT SYSTEM

I don't consider myself a gambler. I play to a strategy not a system. Over the last few years, the face of the compulsive gambler has become an all too familiar sight. I see them with their own 'winning' systems, some of which work for a while, but they never make money in the long term. That is why casinos love them – they are a bread-and-butter source of income. The strategy player is the complete antithesis. I may lose occasionally, but the underlying trend is always upwards.

The only chance I have had to demonstrate my revised strategy was in the Autumn of 1992, when *GQ* magazine arranged for me to play the casinos of northern France. The four-day trip was based on the assumption that I was an unknown quantity in France.

I played at seven casinos and won in six of them. Using my new strategy, I was able to bet more subtly, gradually increasing and decreasing my stake. In five memorable hours at the Grand Casino in Dieppe, I made £1,200, much to the annoyance of the management, who were beside themselves. Once again, they were kind enough to pay for my meal, after which I cashed in my chips and headed for the casino in Deauville.

It all ended dramatically in Enghien les Bains, a casino in the northern suburbs of Paris. It was the last day of my trip and I had turned my original float of £4,000 into £6,000. I had been playing for only twenty minutes, when the manager tapped me on the shoulder and uttered those immortal words. 'Mr O'Brien? We must ask you to leave immediately.' It was not my method of play that betrayed me. They had calculated from my geographical movements that I was a professional player. Why would someone staying at a hotel in Deauville travel to Paris to play blackjack?

THE ROLE OF MEMORY

It is not very easy to adopt my strategy without a trained memory. On a simple level, your overall concentration and powers of observation are so much sharper if you have worked on improving your memory. They need to be: I am often sitting at the table for five or six hours without a break. And in today's casinos, you are being scrutinized from every possible angle. I have quite often found myself playing with three security cameras trained on my table, a croupier watching my every move and an inspector looking over my shoulder!

Most card-counters are easy to spot. They give themselves away by covering their mouths with their hands, trying to conceal lip movements as they frantically struggle to keep count of the cards. They scan the cards with conspicuous head and eye movements, and their play is characterized by long pauses between cards.

I have trained my memory, concentration and observation to the point where I can keep pace with the fastest of dealers, hold a conversation with the inspector and make spontaneous calculations at the same time. I once overheard a croupier in Dieppe observe to a passing inspector, '*Il est trop machine*'. This was an apt description, as I was working robotically.

Memory also plays a vital role when I have to refer back to a mental reference grid that I have compiled. Using location, I can access the print-out from Las Vegas, the books I have read, and my own statistical findings. It is a vast data base, equipping me for every possible hand.

For example, let's assume my first two cards total 12. I immediately refer to a location based around the Peacock Theatre in Woking. (12 = AB. My own person for AB is Alan Bennett, the actor and playwright.) The dealer's card is a 2, which tells me to locate the second stage along the journey: the box office. I have a mental image of bars across the ticket window and the man inside wearing handcuffs, as if he were in a prison. Handcuffs give me a coded true count of +3.

I now know not to draw any more cards if the true count equals or exceeds this level. They are likely to be high, and I could go bust. All guesswork has been completely eliminated from my game. I know there is an optimum decision for every situation, enabling me to act like a robot rather than a gambler.

Next time you visit a casino, look at the man playing blackjack on his own. Look closer still. It might be me!

. . . .

CHAPTER 25

How to beat quiz machines

Soon after I had memorized 7,500 *Trivial Pursuit* questions, it occurred to me that there must be a way of learning the questions on quiz machines found in pubs and clubs. If there were, anyone with a trained memory could make themselves some pocket money.

I looked into the subject and discovered a small group of professional players who tour the country, earning serious amounts of cash. One person, who leaves the initials F.E.Y. on machines, has recently bought a £75,000 house with his earnings. Did he have an exceptional memory?

I decided to meet some of these people to compare notes. Their itinerant lifestyle, moving discreetly from pub to pub, had many similarities with my life as a blackjack card-counter. And we had all spent time committing a large number of trivial questions and answers to memory.

I was encouraged by what I heard. Although the financial rewards aren't as great as blackjack, there is a good living to be had for anyone who has the time and dedication. With a little research, a small investment, and a trained memory, I reckon it is possible to make

£200 cash a day, tax-free, after a few weeks. Needless to say, there is *nothing* illegal about playing quiz machines professionally.

SKILL WITH PRIZES

Quiz machines are known in the trade as SWPS, which stands for 'Skill with Prizes'. Fruit machines are known as AWPS, 'Amusement with Prizes'. Under the current gaming laws, you are allowed to win a maximum of £6 in tokens (£4.80 cash) on an AWP. On an SWP, you can win up to £20 in cash, hence their attraction for professional players.

I have looked into the grey area of 'winning systems' for fruit machines. As far as I can tell, the only advantage to be had is knowing when a machine has recently paid out and satisfied its legal requirements. You can do this by checking the jackpot and bank displays. The recent celebrated case of two teenagers making their fortune on fruit machines owed more to an electronic, highly illegal device for notching up credits without putting in any money. These days, all fruit machines use sophisticated random-number generators that are impossible to predict.

The first quiz machine to appear in Britain was *Quizmaster* in 1985, closely followed by *Give Us A Break* in October 1986, and *Barquest* and *Ten Quid Grid* in 1987. For a while, they became a national obsession. A whole wave of new machines started to appear, many of them based on TV and radio quiz shows. *A Question of Sport, Every Second Counts,*

Strike It Lucky, and *Treble Top* all became market leaders.

Most of them were paying out a top prize of £10. Each machine contained about 1,000 multiple-choice questions; there were three or four answers to choose from, and if you got it wrong, the correct answer was usually given.

The manufacturers were alarmed to discover that SWPS generated considerably less revenue than AWPS. On some sites, they were even losing money, particularly when the prize money went up to £20. It became apparent that they were being targeted by professional players – people who had learnt all the answers.

New editions were hastily brought out, each one containing around 1,000 questions. (At the last count, there were thirty-three editions of *Give Us A Break*!) The professionals learnt them as fast as they appeared. (It was a boom time for the firms that thought up the questions.)

RICH PICKINGS

Today, there are signs that SWP manufacturers have grown tired of trying to outwit the professional player. Machines have been introduced with 10,000 questions, but they have suffered a similar, if slower fate to the others. At the 1993 trade fair for the amusement arcade industry (ATE at Earl's Court in January), there was only one new quiz machine on display: *Brainbox*. It offers a maximum cash prize of £6 and boasts over 12,000 questions. (The questions are generated randomly, and a second data bank of questions can be accessed if too many questions are answered correctly.)

In a dignified retreat, SWP manufacturers have switched the emphasis from large cash prizes to entertainment. The public are given longer on the machine, but they can't win as much. And a new range of machines requiring a completely different set of skills is now coming on to the market. *The Crystal Maze*, a version of the Channel 4 cult TV game, is leading the way.

The implications of all this for professional players are bad in the long term. Manufacturers would clearly like to see the back of the old SWPS that offer £20. However, there is still a huge public demand for these machines (particularly *Give Us A Break, Barquest, Adders and Ladders, Every Second Counts*), and they continue to be installed in their hundreds around Britain's pubs. As these old favourites circulate, there will be rich pickings to be had for the experienced and aspiring player.

THE PROFESSIONALS

Any financial 'sting' requires an initial working capital. To date, most professional players get to know a machine by spending anything up to £250 playing it regularly and memorizing the answers. Simon, a player I met in Brighton (average earnings £400 a week, by no means full-time), wires himself up with a microphone before playing a new machine. Standing in front of it with a couple of friends, he says the answers out loud and transcribes the tape later. (This tactic isn't to be recommended if you are alone!)

However, there is an easier, more systematic way to commit the answers to memory. Every week, World's

Fair Publications publish *Coin Slot International*, a widely read trade paper in the amusement industry. The last half a dozen pages are packed full of advertisements listing second-hand machines for sale, including SWPS.

The paper is little known outside the trade, but it is essential reading for aspiring players. Here is a small selection of some of the SWPS and prices listed in 1993:

Give Us A Break	£150
Snooker Quiz	£175
Adders and Ladders	£145
Barquest	£125
Barquest II	£150
Maze Master	£125
Maze Master II	£125
Every Second Counts	£395

Instead of spending £250 in pubs and clubs, it seems more sensible to buy a second-hand machine from a dealer, play it in the comfort of your own home (the money box can be easily removed) and memorize the answers at leisure. The questions themselves vary quite a lot, but the principles that I outlined in Chapter 17 on *Trivial Pursuit* still apply.

Step 1: Choosing your Machine
Before buying a machine, spend a week going around as many pubs as you can in a chosen area. You will be surprised at how many pubs there are in Britain! (There are 186 in the Hastings area alone.) Find out which machine is the most popular. Freehouses and tenancies tend to hire the old games. Large, brewery-owned pubs are best avoided; they are supplied with

the latest models and the landlords are more vigilant.

Once you have located approximately ten sites where the same machine (and edition) is installed, visit a few dealers, find an identical machine (and edition) and buy it. It might take a little reconnaissance to locate a sufficient number of machines, but it will be worth the effort. Simon plays three editions of his favourite machine in Brighton and three in Worthing.

Step 2: Memorizing the Answers

Once you have installed the machine at home, most of the work has been done. Multiple choice makes life much easier than learning *Trivial Pursuit* questions: if you can't remember the answer, at least you know that it's staring you in the face. There only has to be the faintest association for you to make the link. You should be able to memorize at least two questions a minute.

Remember: isolate a key word in the question and let it suggest a location. Then use an image suggested by the answer. It should be possible to memorize 5,000 questions in thirty-five hours. By my calculation, that's a slightly less than the average working week. And I haven't taken into account the answers that you already know.

Step 3: The Loop

It is important to be subtle as you move around your circuit of chosen pubs (often referred to as a loop). Don't take everything you can out of the first machine; the landlord might not let you in again.

(Professional players make life difficult for landlords, who are often on a profit-share agreement with the machine suppliers.) Buy a drink before you play the machine and try to establish whether it has paid out recently. If someone is playing it, watch how much time they are being given to answer the questions. (Generally speaking, the more time the player has, the more money there is in the machine.)

Once you start to win, make sure it pays out in one thunderous go, preferably when the music is loud and just before you are about to leave. If it is continuously throwing money at you, someone might get suspicious.

You should be able to win between £30 and £50 from each machine before it handicaps itself. Move on the the next pub and don't return for a while. If a machine is being emptied regularly, the landlord might decide to send it back. Milk them slowly!

MORE THAN ONE LOOP

Pubs will swop their machines around after a while and you will have to decide whether to work a new patch or buy a new machine. There is a chance that you will be able to sell your old one back to the dealer or part exchange it. Don't bank on this! Even though there is a demand for SWPS, dealers won't necessarily take them back, and they certainly won't offer you the full price.

Before you buy your first machine, it's sometimes

worth asking the dealer whether they will buy it back from you in a couple of months, but be careful not to arouse their suspicion.

If your initial foray into the world of quiz machines is successful, you should consider investing in more machines. You can then plan a number of loops and alternate between them. There are several advantages. Landlords are less likely to recognize your face if you show up once every month instead of daily. And your revenue will increase!

OTHER PLAYERS

There seems to be a certain amount of co-operation among players. Information is regularly traded about machines, editions, and their various idiosyncrasies (on *Give Us A Break*, edition 7, for example, there is no second chance at the first question). It's fairly easy to spot a professional, and it's always worth having a discreet chat with him or her.

HEALTH WARNING

It is very easy to get out of shape playing quiz machines. The smoky atmosphere of a pub and the constant temptation to drink are not conducive to a healthy lifestyle. Some people play better after one pint of beer. My own experience suggests that the brain performs best without any alcohol. The one thing you must watch out for, however, is the sort of landlord who might get difficult if you order tomato juices all night.

F.E.Y.

The legend of F.E.Y. lives on in pubs around Britain, even though the man himself has now retired from playing. Simon from Brighton first came across the initials F.E.Y. in 1990 in the Lake District, traditionally a happy hunting-ground for professional players. The pubs are small, the tourists provide good cover and the machines are always well stocked with money.

'It was the days when you could leave your initials on the machine if you got a high score,' says Simon. 'I was working in a team with three others. Wherever we went, we found his initials at the top of the all-time highest scores.'

One day Simon walked into a pub in Beverley, Humberside, and to his amazement he saw the initial F.E.Y. at the top of the highest score *of the day*. He looked around, wondering whether, after two years, he had finally caught up with this legendary player.

'I sat in the corner having a pint and waited to see if anyone would play the machine. After twenty minutes, a man came forward and started to play. I knew immediately it was him.'

Simon got chatting with F.E.Y. and compared notes. He was in his early thirties and was about to purchase his £75,000 house. Outside in the car park, F.E.Y. showed him his large van, which he lived in as he travelled the country. He was always on the move.

'It had a shower and I remember noticing all these bulging filofaxes stuffed full of routes, pub names, and questions. He was a graduate, quiet, and, like the best players, had a good general knowledge before he got into the game.'

There aren't many people like F.E.Y., and not many people will want to live his sort of life, but it shows what can be done with a trained memory.

CHAPTER 26

. . . .

Memory and the Greeks

During the course of writing this book, I took the opportunity to read up on the history of memory. It came as something of a shock to discover that there were a number of striking similarities between my method and the Greeks' approach to memory.

I had heard of Simonides of Ceos, the Greek poet born in the sixth century BC, but I had never studied his famous memory skills in detail. A brilliant poet, Simonides is widely acknowledged as the founder of the art of memory.

The Greeks, and later the Romans, went on to develop some of the greatest memories the civilized world has ever seen. Memory was ranked as one of the most important disciplines of oratory, a flourishing art. They were living in an age of no paper, so people couldn't readily refer to any notes. Speeches were committed to memory; lawyers depended on their memory in court; and poets, whose role in society was paramount, regularly drew on their enormous powers of recall to recite long passages of verse.

The Greeks in general had a high level of literacy. Important texts were recorded on papyrus, and wax tablets were used to teach reading and writing in schools. Nevertheless, their culture remained a predominantly oral one.

The classical system disappeared around the fourth century AD, reappeared in the thirteenth century with a religious twist, thanks to Thomas Aquinas and the Scholastics, and adopted various magical, occult, and scientific guises during Medieval and Renaissance times. Sadly, though, the art of memory in Europe had already begun to wane in the fifteenth century with the advent of printing. It put up a heroic fight for almost two centuries but by the end of the seventeenth century, it had become marginalized.

I hope you, too, enjoy discovering the similarities between two systems staring at each other across a divide of over two thousand years. In some ways, it is not so much coincidence, more a case of natural selection: both systems are rooted in personal experience, and have evolved accordingly.

THE DINNER PARTY

The story most people know about Simonides relates to a banquet thrown by a nobleman called Scopas. Simonides chanted a poem in his honour and also included a few verses in praise of Castor and Pollux. When the poet had finished, the slightly jilted host told him that he would only be paid half his fee; he should ask the gods Castor and Pollux for the remainder.

Later on in the meal, a message arrived for Simonides, saying that two men wanted to see him outside. The poet left his table and walked out of the hall.

Moments later, the entire building collapsed, killing everyone inside. Distraught relatives were unable to identify the mutilated corpses, and the authorities had an impossible job working out who had been at the dinner.

Enter Simonides. He had memorized where everyone was sitting and could identify all the corpses. Castor and Pollux had paid back Simonides with interest, but I still prefer being staked £50,000 to play blackjack at Las Vegas.

ARTIFICIAL MEMORY

Much of what we know about Simonides and the classical art of memory comes from three Roman sources, all written between the first century BC and the first century AD: an anonymous work entitled *Ad Herrenium*, Quintilian's *Institutio Oratoria*, and Cicero's *De Oratore*. (The three are discussed in Dame Frances Yates's absorbing book *The Art of Memory*, republished by Pimlico, 1992.) The Romans documented and expanded the practice pioneered by the Greeks.

Written by a teacher, *Ad Herrenium* is addressed to students of rhetoric and concerns itself with the basic rules of memory. In it we learn that the Greeks believed in two types of memory: natural and artificial. Those who are born with good natural memories could improve them still further by training the artificial memory. More significantly, training and exercise could dramatically help anyone who is born with a very poor memory. In other words, however bad it was, your memory could be improved if treated like a muscle and exercised constantly.

'In every discipline,' says the author of *Ad Herrenium*, 'artistic theory is of little avail without unremitting exercise, but especially in mnemonics, theory is almost valueless unless made good by industry, devotion, toil, and care.'

I couldn't have put it better myself!

PLACES

The Greeks discovered that the best way to remember things was to impose order on them. They did this by choosing a series of real places or *loci* which they could visualise in their mind. Images of what they wanted to recall would then be placed on the various *loci*. Writing in *De Oratore*, Cicero says, 'The order of the places will preserve the order of the things to be remembered.'

The Greeks recommended using spacious and architecturally varied buildings. Quintilian suggests using buildings with numerous rooms, forecourts, balconies, arches and statues. 'It is an assistance to the memory,' he writes, 'if places are stamped on the mind, which anyone can believe from experiment. For when we return to a place after a considerable absence, we not merely recognize the place itself, but remember things that we did there, and recall the persons whom we met and even the unuttered thoughts that passed through our minds when we were there before.'

A lot of people might have come across this 'Roman room' method, as it is called; I had heard of positioning literal images around rooms, but always thought it sounded too cramped and confusing. Significantly, Quintilian goes on to say that *loci* don't have to be mapped out around the house: 'What I have spoken of as being done in a house can also be done in public buildings, *or on a long journey* [my italics], or in going through a city.'

This is the only extant text that recommends using journeys. Still, my habit of wandering aimlessly around Guildford, mapping out a mental route, is clearly not so daft after all! Frances Yates even suggests that it would have been common in Greek and Roman times to see lonely students of rhetoric (or poets) meandering around deserted buildings and streets plotting their *loci*. This discovery has serious implications for me: the end of men-in-white-coat jokes. The next time someone stops me in the street and asks with some concern what I am doing, I will look them in the eye and tell them!

RULES FOR PLACES

Loci are compared in *Ad Herrenium* to wax tablets. They can be used again and again, even though the images inscribed on them are regularly wiped off. As befits someone from the twentieth century, I have always described my journeys as blank video tapes, which can be similarly wiped clean and used again.

The Greeks had a number of interesting rules for *loci*. The following are taken from *Ad Herrenium*:

Loci should be deserted or solitary places. Crowds of people tend to weaken impressions and distract from the key image. (Guildford is always a ghost town when I use it as a route.)

The students are urged to give each 5th *locus* a distinguishing mark: they should include a gold hand (five fingers) in the scene, for example. On the 10th *locus*, they should imagine a personal acquaintance called Decimus. (I have always made the 6th, or 11th, or half-way stage stand out in my mind.)

Loci should not be too similar: too many intercolumnar spaces are not recommended, as they might lead to confusion. (I always make sure that my stages are different from each other.)

The intervals between *loci* should be a particular length: thirty feet.

The *loci* should be not too large, or too small, too brightly lit, or too dark.

Imaginary places can be used as well as real. It is also good to mix both together: give your house an extra floor, etc.

IMAGES

The Greeks had two types of images; one for memorizing things, arguments, or notions; and one for remembering single words. Each image would be placed at a different *locus*. As he was reciting his poetry, Simonides would have moved around his mental journey, recalling each image as he went. Lawyers would remind themselves of the details of a case in this way; orators would know their next subject or topic. (Interestingly, the English word 'topic' comes from the Greek *topos*, which means place or *locus*.)

The second type of imagery, for individual words, seems a little extreme. Most Latin sources are in agreement that the idea of referring to a new *locus* for each word of a speech was preposterous. The author of *Ad Herrenium* suggests that it was, at best, a good mental exercise.

THE USE OF PEOPLE

According to the author of *Ad Herrenium*, certain images stick in the mind, others don't; adopting the tone of a psychologist, he sets out to find the most memorable image.

'If we see or hear something exceptionally base, dishonourable, unusual, great, unbelievable, or ridiculous, we are likely to remember it for a long time. We ought then to set up images of a kind that can adhere longest in memory.

And we shall do so if we establish similitudes as striking as possible; if we set up images that are not many or vague but *active* [my italics]; if we assign to them exceptional beauty or singular ugliness; if we ornament some of them, as with crowns or purple cloaks, or if we somehow disfigure them, as by introducing one stained with blood, or soiled with mud, or smeared with red paint, so that its form is more striking, or by assigning certain comic effects to our images, for that too will ensure our remembering them more readily.'

FURTHER EVIDENCE

I find this passage from *Ad Herrenium* particularly uncanny. As you know, people play an essential part in my approach to memory. I have even assigned characters to every number from 00 to 99. *Ad Herrenium* is the only one of the three surviving Latin sources which states that people make the best images. Quintilian advocates the use of objects such as anchors (to remind him of the naval content of a speech) and weapons (to remind him of the military content), and Cicero talks ambiguously about using masks (persona) as images.

It won't surprise you to learn that I think *Ad Herrenium* is the most accurate account of the Greeks' use of imagery. The famous anecdote about Simonides and the banquet suggests that he was equally adept at memorizing people as he was places, or *loci*. There is also an extant fragment of Greek text (Dialexeis, 400 BC) which implies that the Greeks thought of the hero Achilles to remember courage, and Hephaestus to remember metal working.

Thomas Aquinas's chief contribution to the art of memory was to establish it in a religious context. In the hands of the thirteenth-century Scholastics, memory shifted from rhetoric to ethics, even becoming a part of the cardinal virtue of Prudence. Put simply, memory was a way of getting to heaven and avoiding hell. Virtues and vices were quickly personified; once they were seen as people, we all stood a better chance of remembering what was right and wrong in this world.

THE IMPORTANCE OF ACTIONS

The passage from *Ad Herrenium* illustrates another similarity between our two systems. The emphasis on active images (*imagines agentes*) is identical; I have always stressed that each person must have a unique and distinguishing action, and here Simonides is saying that the image must be doing something.

There are only three examples of human images in *Ad Herrenium*. This is a pity, although I applaud the reason why the author didn't leave us with more. As I have stressed all along in this book, the best images are the ones that you make up for yourself. The author of *Ad Herrenium* took a similar line, stating his task as tutor was not to list a thousand examples, but to teach the method, give a couple of illustrations, and let the student do the rest.

Those images that we do have are, nevertheless, fine examples. In the same way that I asked you, when remembering a long number, to combine a person with the action to create a complex image, so the author of *Ad Herrenium* urges the student to throw together a number of different images.

In the following example, he chooses an image that a lawyer might use when remembering details about a case: the defendant has poisoned a man, the motive was to gain an inheritance, and there were numerous witnesses.

'We shall imagine the man in question as lying ill in bed, if we know him personally. If we do not know him, we shall take someone to be our invalid, so that he may come to mind at once. And we shall place the defendant at the bedside, holding in his right hand a cup, in his left, tablets, and on the fourth finger, a ram's testicles. In this way we can have in memory the man who was poisoned, the witnesses, and the inheritance.'

This complex image would be placed at the first *locus*. The cup would remind the lawyer of the poison; and the tablets, the inheritance. The lawyer could, in this way, remember the pertinent details of the case. Further, related information would be stored in similar form at the second *locus*, and so on. In effect, the lawyer is using his *loci* as a mental filing cabinet.

It is also worth noting here, although it is not as clear as it could be in this passage, that the author of *Ad Herrenium* is suggesting that we use people we know personally.

SOUNDS SIMILAR

The ram's testicles are a more unusual aspect of the image. Frances Yates, in her discussion on the subject, suggests that the Latin word for testicle (*testiculus*) would have reminded the lawyer of the word for witnesses (*testis*). In another part of *Ad Herrenium*, she points out, the author gives an example of an image ('Domitius raising his hands to heaven while he is lashed by the Marcii Reges') that is designed to remind the student of rhetoric of a particular sentence ('*domum itionem reges*'). The only obvious connection is in the sound of the words. I subscribe to this interpretation. When I am memorizing someone's name, for example, I often use images that include something that sounds similar to the person's name.

The reason why the testicles must belong to a ram is less clear; Yates suggests that it has something to do with Aries and the signs of the Zodiac, the order of which was known to have been used as a mnemonic.

IMAGINATION

Practitioners of the classical art of memory must have had an extraordinarily vivid inner vision. Anyone who comments on the lighting of a particular *locus* along an imaginary route is assuming tremendous powers of imagery. Simonides himself was universally praised for his use of evocative imagery in his poetry, and he frequently compared his poems to paintings.

Aristotle (fourth century BC), writing in *De Anima*, believed that the human soul never thought without first creating a mental picture. All knowledge and information entered the soul via the five senses; the imagination would act upon it first, turning the information into images; only then could the intellect get to work.

Aristotle's theory of knowledge has an important bearing on memory, although he himself was never a great believer in the mnemonics practised by Simonides. In Chapter 2, I said that the key to a good memory was your imagination. Even though he might have disapproved of much of this book, Aristotle would not have found fault there.

Memory, he argued, belonged to the same part of the soul as the imagination. Both faculties were concerned with the forming of images; there was simply a small time difference: memory dealt with things past, rather than with things present.

Our understanding of the imagination is slightly different today, but its similarities with memory are still there for all to see. They are two sides of the same coin, both requiring inner vision.

LAWS OF ASSOCIATION

Aristotle is often attributed with forming the laws of association. We remember something by recalling something else that is similar, closely related, or opposite to that which we want to remember. Clearly, this is the basis of every memory system ever invented, not just mine. If we can't remember the actual name, object, number, or topic, we recall something else (a place or image), which then triggers off our memory.

Aristotle makes this point when he is discriminating between reminiscence and memory in *De Anima*. He goes on to say that those things that are the easiest to remember have an order, a theory we have already discussed.

Loci, images, actions, persons, imagination, association, order – it's no wonder the Greeks had such good memories.

CHAPTER 27

. . . .

Famous memory men

There have been a number of famous memory men throughout the ages, ranging from Simonides in the sixth century BC to Leslie Welch in the 1950s. Some were professional mnemonists, earning a living from their skills; others used memory for grander ends, such as understanding the universe. In this chapter, I describe twelve of the best-known memory men. Most of them had trained memories; a few were born with more inexplicable powers.

METRODORUS OF SCEPSIS

Metrodorus was a Greek man of letters, who turned away from philosophy to pursue a political life and to teach rhetoric. He lived in the first century BC and was a worthy successor to Simonides, widely considered as the founder of the art of memory. (For more on Simonides, see Chapter 26.)

One of Metrodorus's favourite tricks was to memorize conversations. Later on, he would repeat them back to people, verbatim. We think he did this by employing shorthand images for words or groups of words. (Sadly, his written works have all been lost.)

Instead of using a journey, Metrodorus placed

images in the zodiac. He divided up the twelve signs (Aries, Taurus, etc) into thirty-six decans, each one represented by thirty-six associated images. In turn, he used every degree (all 360 of them) as a stage (*locus*), providing him with one long and ordered journey.

PETER OF RAVENNA

Peter of Ravenna was a fifteenth-century entrepreneur who spotted a gap in the market for mnemonics. Trained as jurist in Padua, he published a memory book in 1491, which in today's terms was an international bestseller. *The Phoenix* was translated into many languages, went through numerous editions and was considered a bible for anyone who wanted to improve their memory.

Peter removed memory from the religious context that Thomas Aquinas and the thirteenth-century Scholastics had given it, and set about introducing mnemonics to the lay masses. He encouraged people to look out for suitable journeys on their pilgrimages and recommended the use of sexual images. The practical handbook was publicized by his own memory feats: he memorized 20,000 legal points, 200 speeches of Cicero, and the entire canon law. (Give me *Trivial Pursuit* any day.)

GIULO CAMILLO

Camillo was one of the most famous men in the sixteenth century. Largely forgotten now, he was known at the time as the 'divine Camillo'. His fame spread throughout Italy and France, thanks entirely to a creation of his known as a 'memory theatre'. Initially financed by the king of France, Camillo set about building a wooden model theatre, big enough for two people to enter. He claimed that it contained everything the human mind could conceive.

We know that Camillo was a neo-platonist and believed in archetypes, but sadly he never got around to writing down in detail the theory behind his memory theatre. Furthermore, he had a terrible stutter and his explanations weren't as intelligible as they might have been.

The celebrated wooden theatre caused a stir wherever Camillo took it. On one occasion in Paris, his awesome reputation was further enhanced by a trip to see some wild animals. A lion escaped, scattering people in all directions. Camillo stood his ground, and the animal walked slowly around him, even caressing him, until a keeper chased it back to its cage.

The theatre itself was based on some of the classical principles of memory. Its purpose was to help people remember the entire universe; information and ideas were translated into images, and 'placed' in ordered points (*loci*) around the auditorium.

The individual stood on the stage and looked out at the images. The most important information (the planets) was 'seated', appropriately enough, in the stalls; the cheaper seats contained less significant data, graded according to their place in the order of creation.

GIORDANO BRUNO

Bruno started off in life as a Dominican friar, and ended up being burnt at the stake in 1600. (Such are the hazards of the job.) In between times, he was an Italian philosopher. Twentieth-century admirers of his work include James Joyce, who made occasional references to 'the Nolan', which baffled his friends. (Bruno was born in Nola.)

Bruno joined the Dominican order when he was fifteen, and familiarized himself with the classical art of memory, through the works of Thomas Aquinas. He soon became widely known for his memory skills and performed in front of the pope, among others, before quitting the order.

As Camillo had done before him, he went to France, where he promised to reveal his memory secrets to the king (Henri III). To show willing, he dedicated his first book on memory to the king. *De Umbris Idearum* is another attempt to order the entire universe, thereby making it more memorable and understandable. It consists of a series of imaginary rotating 'memory wheels' and is mind-bogglingly complicated.

Frances Yates, an expert on the Renaissance magical tradition, has bravely pieced together this extraordinary concept (*The Art of Memory*, Chapter 9). She suggests that there was a central wheel containing the signs of the Zodiac, which worked the other wheels, each of which was divided up into 150 images! As far as I can gather, there were five wheels in total; they rotated like a kaleidoscope, generating any number of images.

MATTEO RICCI

Ricci was a sixteenth-century Italian Jesuit missionary who dedicated his life to converting the Chinese to Catholicism. Using principles that he attributed to Simonides, he trained his mind to create vast memory palaces. Concepts, people, objects could all be stored in these mental buildings if they were translated into images and placed inside.

Ever the ingenious missionary, he performed endless feats of memory, hoping that the Chinese would want to discover more about the religion of such a gifted man. He could recite a list of 500 Chinese ideograms and repeat them in reverse order. If he were given a volume from a Chinese classic, he could repeat it after one brief reading. (Ricci probably studied under Francesco Panigarola in Rome, who was able to 'walk' around over 100,000 placed images.)

More craftily, he encouraged his Chinese students to remember the tenth position of a journey by including the ideograph for 'ten' in their image, which happened to be in the shape of a crucifix.

In 1596, twelve years after he had settled in China, he wrote a short book on memory in Chinese, and donated it to Lu Wangai, the Governor of Jiangxi. Lu's three sons were studying for government exams. They had to pass them if they were to make a success of their lives. Ricci's book was a timely introduction to mnemonics, which they could use while studying.

S

One of the most analysed memories this century belonged to a Russian called Shereshevsky, otherwise known as S. He aspired to be a violinist, became a journalist and ended up earning his living as a professional mnemonist. According to the famous neuropsychologist Professor Luria, who studied S over a period of thirty years, there were no distinct limits to his memory.

Luria presented him with 70-digit matrices, complex scientific formulae, even poems in foreign languages, all of which he could memorize in a matter of minutes. He was even able to recall the information perfectly fifteen years later.

S's experience of the world around him was quite different from ours. He was born with a condition known as synaesthesia: the stimulation of one sense produces a reaction in another. (Alexander Scriabin the composer was also synaesthetic. The condition is often induced by hallucinogenic drugs.)

In S's case, he automatically translated the world around him into vivid mental images that lasted for years. He couldn't help but have a good memory. If he was asked to memorize a word, he would not only hear it, but he would also see a colour. On some occasions, he would also experience a taste in his mouth and a feeling on his skin. Later on, when he was asked to repeat the word, he had a number of triggers to remind him.

He also used images to remember numbers:

'Take the number 1. This is a proud, well-built man;

2 is a high-spirited woman; 3 a gloomy person (why, I don't know); 6 a man with a swollen foot; 7 a man with a moustache; 8 a very stout woman – a sack within a sack. As for the number 87, what I see is a fat woman and a man twirling his moustache.'

Synaesthesia created problems in other areas of his life. The sound of a word would often generate an image quite different from the word's meaning:

'One time I went to buy some ice cream . . . I walked over to the vender and asked her what kind of ice cream she had. 'Fruit ice cream,' she said. But she answered in such a tone that a whole pile of coals, of black cinders, came bursting out of her mouth, and I couldn't bring myself to buy any ice cream after she had answered in that way . . . Another thing: if I read when I eat, I have a hard time understanding what I am reading – the taste of the food drowns out the sense.'

Metaphors, idioms, poetry (particularly Boris Pasternak), anything that wasn't literal in meaning was hard for him to grasp. If he had spoken English, for example, and you had accused him of 'driving a hard bargain', he would have been overwhelmed with images, not all of them very helpful. Driving a car . . . something hard like a rock . . . a scene in a market.

If he couldn't visualize something, he was stumped. His wife had to explain what 'nothing' meant. And reading was a problem, because of all the images that the words generated. 'Other people, think as they read, but I see it all. The things I see when I read aren't real, they don't fit the context.'

Needless to say, S had a phenomenal imagination. Luria believed that he spent a large part of his life living in the world of his images. As a child, he would visualize the hands on his clock staying at 7.30 so he could stay in bed. He could increase his pulse from 70 beats a minute to 100, simply by imagining he was running for a train. In one experiment, he raised the temperature of his left hand and lowered the temperature of the other (both by two degrees) just by imagining he had one hand on a stove while the other was holding a block of ice. He could even get his pupils to contract by imagining a bright light!

For a while, the only way he could forget images was by writing them down and burning the paper, but he could still see the letters in the embers. Towards the end of his life he realized he could forget things only if he had a conscious desire to erase them.

Ironically, people's faces were a constant source of trouble.

'They're so changeable. A person's expression depends on his mood and on the circumstances under which you happen to meet him. People's faces are constantly changing; it's the different shades of expression that confuse me and make it so hard to remember faces.'

Finally, a brief word about his use of random location.

When he first became a mnemonist, and had to memorize a list of words, he would 'visit' a place that was associated with each word. He appeared to have no control over his mental movements, toing and froing everywhere.

'I had just started out from Mayakovsky Square when they gave me the word 'Kremlin', so I had to get myself off to the Kremlin. Okay, I can throw a rope across to it . . . But right after that they gave me the word 'poetry' and once again I found myself on Pushkin Square. If I had been given 'American Indian', I'd have had to get to America. I could, of course, throw a rope across the ocean, but it's so exhausting travelling . . .'

Later, he began to use regular journeys and placed each image at a particular point. Just as the Greeks had recommended over two thousand years earlier, he appreciated the need for well-lit scenes and would often erect street lamps above images if they were on a dark stretch of his journey.

(For anyone who wants to know more about the fascinating life of S, I recommend Professor Luria's absorbing book *The Mind of a Mnemonist*.)

IRENO FUNES

The sole documentor of the unusual life of Ireno Funes was the Argentine writer Jorge Luis Borges, which will set the alarm bells ringing in anyone who is concerned solely with historical truths. Borges enjoyed mixing fact with fiction in his writing, developing a style that came to be known as magical realism. His account of Funes is found in *Ficciónes*, a collection of short stories that, as the title suggests, owed more than a little to Borges' imagination.

However, it is more than likely that Funes was based on someone Borges knew, or had heard about. We know that other characters in Borges' work were modelled on people drawn from real life. Having said that, there are some patent absurdities in his account, which I will come to later.

Borges is not sure who Funes's parents were, but his father might have been an Englishman called O'Connor. He lived in Fray Bentos (of corned beef fame) and was known for his ability to tell the time without consulting a watch. Borges visited him twice. On the second occasion he learnt that when Funes was nineteen years old, had fallen off his horse, crippling him for life. The near fatal accident, however, had a plus side: he woke up with a perfect memory!

Funes could suddenly recall every day of his life, and even claimed to remember the cloud formation on a particular day five years earlier. (This is something that I find a little hard to believe; his ability to compare the formation with water spray before the 'battle of Quebracho' smacks of pure literary invention.) He learnt English, French, Portuguese, and Latin with ease, and dismissed his physical disabilities as unimportant in the light of his exceptional memory.

On close examination of the text, it would appear that Borges is presenting us with an accurate case study of someone who had synaesthesia, coupled with a heightened sense of visual imagery – just like S, in fact. 'We, in a glance, perceive three wine glasses on the table,' writes Borges; 'Funes saw all the shoots, clusters, and grapes of the vine.' Borges describes a man whose senses picked up the minutest details about the world (which were then stored in his memory), but who was 'incapable of general, platonic ideas'.

In a passage uncannily similar to Luria's account of S, Borges describes Funes's perception of 'the many faces of a dead man during a protracted wake'. He was even surprised by the sight of himself in a mirror. Remembering faces wasn't easy for someone who could detect the minutest changes in expression, colour and feeling. It's this sort of psychological detail that makes me think Borges based his account on a real person.

Funes had also developed his own system for memorizing numbers. It comes as no surprise to learn that he translated them into people and other memorable symbols. For example, 7017 became 'Maximo Perez'; the year 1714 became 'the train'; Napoleon meant another number (Borges doesn't specify which – he was clearly mystified by the system); Agustin de Vedia another.

On discovering his exceptional talent, Funes set about cataloguing every memory image from his life: 70,000 of them by his calculation. In its breadth of ambition, the project is reminiscent of Renaissance attempts (Bruno and Camillo) to catalogue all human knowledge. Sadly, Funes died of a pulmonary congestion at the age of twenty-one.

V.P.

Born in Latvia (near the birthplace of S), V.P. (his case file doesn't disclose his name) had memorized 150 poems by the age of ten. He was brought up in an East European Jewish culture, where there was a strong oral tradition. Great emphasis was placed on learning things by rote. V.P. emigrated to the United States, where he worked as a store clerk, and earned a certain amount of notoriety by his ability to play seven chess games simultaneously, wearing a blindfold.

He could speak English, Latvian, German, and Russian fluently and had a reading knowledge of all modern European languages, with the exception of Greek and Hungarian. But it would be quite wrong to describe V.P. as an intellectual genius. He had an IQ of 136.

In 1972, he was the subject of a study by the psychologists E. Hunt and T. Love, who concluded that his memory of words owed a lot to linguistic and semantic associations. He was usually able to find a word in another language that sounded similar to, or had some connection with, the word he wanted to memorize.

PROFESSOR A.C. AITKEN

A.C. Aitken was a professor of mathematics at the University of Edinburgh. He was one of those people who could make lightning-fast, complex mathematical calculations in his head. Although he was first and foremost a mathematician, his unusual memory skills deserve a mention.

He once memorized the first 1,000 digits of pi and said it was like 'learning a Bach fugue'. It would appear that he arranged the digits in rows of fifty, each row comprising ten groups of five numbers. He would then read through them, adopting a certain rhythm.

When it came to reciting the digits, he would call out five per second, followed by a pause, and then another five digits. In this way, he would get through fifty digits every fifteen seconds.

His familiarity with numbers helped him to translate them into more memorable forms. When confronted with 1961, for example, he immediately saw 37×53, or $44^2 + 5^2$, or $40^2 + 19^2$.

LESLIE WELCH

Leslie Welch is perhaps the best-known Memory Man of all. Often referred to as a walking sports encyclopaedia, he became famous for his ability to answer almost any question on football, horse racing and cricket. He played to packed music halls in the late 1940s and 1950s, bewildering audiences wherever he went. Millions tuned in to his radio shows and he was soon earning £11,000 a year. Then it all went wrong. He ended his working life as a £25-a-week accountant for the Department of Employment.

Welch was fascinated with facts and figures. At the age of four, he was reading Wisden's *Cricketers' Almanac* and *Ruff's Guide to the Turf*. He matriculated with honours from Latimer School, Edmonton, in history and mathematics, astounding examiners with the breadth and detail of his knowledge.

During the war, he was a tank commander with the Eighth Army in the Western Desert. One evening, his Regimental Sergeant Major got into a furious argument with another soldier about who won a Manchester Derby in the 1930s. Welch intervened in his inimitable cockney way. 'Excuse me Sergeant Major, City won 3–1, goals scored by Tilson (2) and Herd. The teams were . . .'. Whereupon he proceeded to rattle out both line-ups.

In 1944, he was transferred to ENSA to entertain the troops with his memory skills. After being de-mobbed in 1946, he had his own radio slot, broadcasting to 15 million people on *Calling All Forces*. By 1952, he had a show on Radio Luxembourg called *Beat the Memory Man*. Sponsored by Bovril, the programme invited listeners to phone in on air to ask him questions. They got a guinea if he answered correctly, £25 if they caught him out.

Welch estimated that he was asked over one million questions in his life. He made eleven short films with Twentieth-Century Fox, appeared in 4,000 radio programmes, 500 TV shows and eight Royal Command Performances. So what went wrong?

In the late 1950s, bookings dried up. By 1960, he was a finance officer at the Holloway branch of the Department of Employment. On his retirement in 1972, he tried to make a come-back, landing a regular spot on Radio 2's *Late Night Extra*. The switchboards were jammed with listeners trying to call in, but the memory man was soon forgotten. He died on 8 February 1980, aged seventy-three.

He once gave a very revealing interview to Ian Gilchrist of the *Sunday Express*, in which he talked at length about the abrupt end to his career. Nodding towards his wife, Kathleen, who was sitting in the garden as they spoke, he gave this assessment of his career's untimely end.

'It was her, see. She was my biggest problem. When I started on the radio, she didn't want me to do this for a living. No, she wanted me to be at home at night. But things moved too quickly for her to stop them. The show was a hit straight away.

'About 1957, the wife says, "Look, our two girls have married, we've got this house, just the two of us, and you're not going to leave me alone at night any more."

'Well, I like my home comforts, see. I sat on my bottom for three years, during which I finished up being seven or eight thousand pounds worse off. The number of bookings I turned down was nobody's business. I had to decide whether to sacrifice my home life by going around the Northern clubs, or whether to take a safe nine-to-five job.

'The wife and I are opposites in many ways. And maybe that's why we've stayed together for forty years. She's a worry-guts, a pessimist. She dies a thousand deaths when I'm on stage. But she's been a very dominant influence in my life and I'm not going to sacrifice that for the sake of earning five or six hundred up North.

'Anyway, have you ever been to any of these Northern clubs? People I was once proud to work with, household names, now go up and do fifteen minutes of sheer concentrated filth. I don't want to follow that sort of act. I still consider myself at the top. There isn't a better known speciality act in the country than yours truly.'

HARRY LORAYNE

Harry Lorayne is one of the great memory men of the twentieth century – a fine performer, actor and lecturer. Hundreds of companies, including the likes of IBM, US Steel and General Electric, have hired him to conduct seminars on mind power and memory training. And he has appeared on just about every American TV show, including Johnny Carson's *The Tonight Show*, *Good Morning America*, and *The Today Show*.

Lorayne grew up in the depression years of the late 1920s and 1930s, in New York's Lower East Side. After dropping out of high school because his family had no money, he held a number of errand and clerking jobs, all of them low paid. In World War II, he ended up working in the Army accounting office because of his aptitude for figures. There he met and married his present wife and decided to go into showbusiness at the end of the war.

Ever since the age of eight, he had been fascinated by magic. (He has written fifteen books for other magicians and is a highly respected teacher.) He began to play small nightclubs in New York, where his exceptional skills began to be noticed. Once or twice, he introduced simple memory feats, which seemed to go down well, even better than the magic. He decided to read every book he could find on memory. After months of being holed up in the public library, he emerged with the beginnings of his own system.

'Out of knowledge, trial and error – especially error at first – I began to work on a memory system of my own. I used it myself, at first. It worked. Those memory demonstrations went into my act. I found that they were the highlights. I began to decrease the magic until finally I was doing all memory and no magic.'

Still in his twenties, he found himself on network television. America, it seems, couldn't get enough of him, and he went on to have a phenomenal career. His books are widely read in Britain, but Lorayne as a performer is not so well known; some people might remember his appearance on Michael Parkinson's TV chat show in the 1970s.

The walls of his office today are covered with letters from people all around the world who have benefited from his approach to memory. One is from the Academy Award-winning actress Anne Bancroft, who uses his techniques for learning scripts; another is from a prisoner of war.

'We relied on your memory systems for sanity. We

applied them and learned literally thousands of foreign words, poems, speeches, mathematics, electronics, classical music, philosophy, the list is endless. Just wanted to tell you how much your systems meant to all of us in captivity.'

TONY BUZAN

Tony Buzan is one of the leading world authorities on brain power. He lectures all around the world, advising royalty, governments, multi-nationals such as BP, Digital Equipment Corporation, General Motors and Rank Xerox, and universities.

His most important contribution to date has been 'Mindmapping', a very successful method of ordering information in a visual way. A subject is broken down into its component parts and displayed on a page in different colours, allowing you to see and make new connections.

Buzan has also written extensively on memory. He is chairman of the Brain Club, an international organization designed to increase mental, physical and spiritual awareness, and he has also edited the *International Journal Of Mensa* (the high IQ society's magazine). Born in London in 1942, he emigrated to Vancouver in 1954 and graduated from the University of Colombia in 1964 with double honours in Psychology, English, Maths and General Sciences. He has lived in England since 1966. In 1991, he set up the first ever World MEMORIAD with Raymond Keene, chess correspondent of *The Times*.

CHAPTER 28

. . . .

Conclusion

I hope that you have enjoyed reading this book and that you are already putting some of the methods into practice. Don't try doing too much in one go; see it as a training programme. An athlete, after all, doesn't get fit overnight, and your brain is like a very sensitive and powerful muscle. A little bit of practice every day is much better than a burst of activity followed by frustration. Practice makes a perfect memory.

Apart from the basic principle of using a mental journey, there is one particular aspect of this book that I would like you to take away and use immediately in your everyday life: the DOMINIC SYSTEM. This makes the world an easier place to remember; without it you won't fully reap the benefits of a trained memory. It plays a central role in the mental diary, speeches, history, geography, cards, job interviews, appointments. Numbers are everywhere and it's worth spending time on a system that makes them accessible and memorable.

The DOMINIC SYSTEM is a language, but you will only be communicating with yourself. Let it adapt to your own needs and idiosyncrasies. I have given examples to show you the basic grammar, but you must develop your own patois and vocabulary. The system makes the unintelligible world of numbers intelligible. What makes sense to you might be garbage to me, but if it works, use it.

I said at the beginning of this book that you would be asked to create a lot of strange and bizarre images. Don't be overwhelmed by the sheer number my method requires. They are, I believe, the best way of storing information in your head, providing you use your imagination. Your memory loves images. There are few filing systems in the world that could match the brain for size or efficiency, when images are used in conjunction with a journey.

Don't forget my whole approach to memory has adapted and evolved over time. Yours must do the same. I have showed you the basic principles. Apply them and you are well on the way to developing a perfect memory. Good luck!

BIBLIOGRAPHY

A.A.A., *Beat the Machines! How to Play Quiz Machines and Win*, (Stranger Games 1990).

Alan D. Baddeley, *The Psychology of Memory*, (Harper & Row 1976).

Jorge Luis Borges, *Fictions*, trans. Anthony Kerrigan (Weidenfeld and Nicolson 1942).

G.H. Bower and M.B. Karlin, 'Depth of Processing Pictures of Faces and Recognition Memory', *Journal of Experimental Psychology*, 103 (1974) pp. 751 – 7.

H.E. Butler, translation of *Institutio Oratoria*, (Loeb 1954).

Tony Buzan, *Use Your Memory*, (BBC 1986).

H. Caplan, translation of *Ad Herrenium*, (Leob 1954).

E. Hunt and T. Love, 'How Good Can Memory Be?', in *Coding Processes in Human Memory*, (Winston/Wiley 1972) pp. 237-60.

Harry Lorayne, *How to Develop a Super Power Memory*, (Thorsons 1986).

A.R. Luria, *The Mind of a Mnemonist*, (Harvard University Press 1987).

Sheila Ostrander and Lunn Schroeder, *Cosmic Memory*, (Souvenir Press 1992).

R.N. Shepard, 'Recognition Memory for Words, Sentences and Pictures', *Journal of Experimental Psychology*, 81 (1969) pp. 156-63.

Alastair G. Smith, *Anatomy Mnemonics*, (Churchill Livingstone 1972).

Jonathan D. Spence, *The Memory Palaces of Matteo Ricci*, (Faber 1986).

Susan Stetler, *Actors, Artists, Authors and Attempted*

275

Assassins, *The Almanac of Famous and Infamous People*, (Visible Ink Press 1991).

E.W. Sutton and H. Rackam, translation of *De Oratore*, (Loeb 1954).

Mary Warnock, *Memory*, (Faber 1987).

Frances Yates, *The Art of Memory*, (Pimlico 1992).

R. Yin, 'Looking at Upside-down Faces', *Journal of Experimental Psychology*, 81 (1969) pp. 141 – 5.

TEST YOUR BUSINESS SKILLS

J. MAYA PILKINGTON

THE ESSENTIAL GUIDE
TO ASSESSING YOUR BUSINESS SKILLS

**Do you have what it takes
to be a success in business?**

TEST YOUR BUSINESS SKILLS

consists of a series of carefully chosen tests –
so that you can assess your suitability for a
particular career, and your skills in carrying
out your job.

★ **Does your job suit your talents?**

★ **What's your management style?**

★ **Do you have executive skills?**

★ **What's causing a hold-up to your ambitions?**

★ **Do you have drive and persistence?**

The tests in this book will give you all the
answers to these and many other vital questions
– and not only help you to appreciate your own
abilities, but show you how to achieve greater
success in business.

NON-FICTION/BUSINESS   0 7472 3915 0

More Non-Fiction from Headline:

JUST THE ONE

THE WIVES AND TIMES OF
JEFFREY BERNARD

G R A H A M   L O R D

'One of the most thoroughly researched biographical enquiries I have read. It's all here, booze, women, Norman Balon, horses, "No-knickers Joyce", booze, and finally fame of a sort a writer rarely achieves in his lifetime' Patrick Marnham, *The Oldie*

Jeffrey Bernard, the legendary Soho journalist and boozer who has been popping down to the pub for 'just the one' for forty years is the most unlikely hero of our times.

What other bottle-of-vodka-and-fifty-fags-a-day hack has also been a gigolo, navvy, fairground boxer, miner, stagehand, film editor and actor? Who else has been married four times, seduced 500 lovers (including several renowned actresses) – and also written a famous column for the *Spectator*, his 'suicide note in weekly instalments'? In the astonishingly successful stage play, *Jeffrey Bernard is Unwell*, his rackety life has been portrayed by Peter O'Toole, Tom Conti, James Bolam and Dennis Waterman.

Graham Lord – who has known Bernard well for many years – has written a biography that is fun, devastatingly frank and critical, yet unexpectedly touching. Jeffrey Bernard is indeed unique – just the one.

'I wanted it to be longer. I read it from cover to cover in one sitting and laughed out loud and often' Paul Pickering, *Sunday Times*

'A gripping and unsentimental biography... an astonishing achievement' Irma Kurtz, *Sunday Express*

NON-FICTION/BIOGRAPHY   0 7472 4286 0

—— BARBARA KAFKA ——
MICROWAVE GOURMET
THE DEFINITIVE MICROWAVE COOKBOOK

'An extraordinary, comprehensive book'
Jane Grigson, *Observer*

What do you use *your* microwave for?

To warm up coffee? Defrost bread from the freezer? Heat up
ready-prepared supermarket meals? Bake a potato or two?

Yes, but what else can it do?

In this definitive guide to microwave cooking, Barbara Kafka
shows, with a dazzling combination of culinary flair and
scientific exactitude, how, by using a little care and
imagination, you can make delicious meals out of fresh
ingredients quickly and efficiently.

With over 600 recipes, a comprehensive dictionary of foods
and techniques and advice on what the microwave can and
cannot do, *Microwave Gourmet* covers everything from such
basics as vegetable stock through classic dishes like Moules
Marinières to rich dinner-party fare. Using precise easy-to-
follow instructions, Barbara Kafka explains how to cook
Paupiettes of Sole Stuffed with Salmon in three minutes,
plum jam in thirteen minutes and artichokes in seven. As she
herself says, 'It may not be a mystic experience, but it sure is
quick and efficient.' Whether you are a beginner or an
experienced microwave cook, *Microwave Gourmet* will prove
to be as indispensable as your microwave itself.

'I feel fairly certain that it will make all other books on
microwave cookery redundant' Paul Levy, *Observer*

'This intelligent person's guide to the microwave . . . is long
overdue' *Sunday Times*

'The book I've turned to again and again has been Barbara
Kafka's *Microwave Gourmet*' Sophie Grigson,
Evening Standard

'This stupendously good book' *Cosmopolitan*

NON-FICTION/COOKERY   0 7472 3380 2

A selection of non-fiction from Headline

THE *INDEPENDENT* BOOK OF ANNIVERSARIES	George Beal	£8.99 ☐
MEAN BEANS	Cas Clarke	£5.99 ☐
ENCYCLOPEDIA OF FORENSIC SCIENCE	Brian Lane	£7.99 ☐
JUST THE ONE: The Wives and Times of Jeffrey Bernard	Graham Lord	£6.99 ☐
MALE SEXUAL AWARENESS	Barry McCarthy	£5.99 ☐
BURNS: A Biography of Robert Burns	James Mackay	£8.99 ☐
WORLD ENCYCLOPEDIA OF 20TH CENTURY MURDER	Jay Robert Nash	£8.99 ☐
PLAYFAIR FOOTBALL ANNUAL 1993-94	Jack Rollin (Ed)	£3.99 ☐
HEART AND SOLE	David Sole with Derek Douglas	£5.99 ☐

All Headline books are available at your local bookshop or newsagent, or can be ordered direct from the publisher. Just tick the titles you want and fill in the form below. Prices and availability subject to change without notice.

Headline Book Publishing PLC, Cash Sales Department, Bookpoint, 39 Milton Park, Abingdon, OXON, OX14 4TD, UK. If you have a credit card you may order by telephone – 0235 831700.

Please enclose a cheque or postal order made payable to Bookpoint Ltd to the value of the cover price and allow the following for postage and packing:
UK & BFPO: £1.00 for the first book, 50p for the second book and 30p for each additional book ordered up to a maximum charge of £3.00.
OVERSEAS & EIRE: £2.00 for the first book, £1.00 for the second book and 50p for each additional book.

Name ....

Address ....

....

....

If you would prefer to pay by credit card, please complete:
Please debit my Visa/Access/Diner's Card/American Express (delete as applicable) card no:

Signature .... Expiry Date ....